HOW TO CLIMB® SERIES

Climbing Anchors Field Guide

Third Edition

John Long
and Bob Gaines

FALCONGUIDES

ESSEX, CONNECTICUT

FALCONGUIDES®

An imprint of Globe Pequot, the trade division of
The Rowman & Littlefield Publishing Group, Inc.
4501 Forbes Blvd., Ste. 200
Lanham, MD 20706
www.rowman.com

Falcon and FalconGuides are registered trademarks and Make Adventure Your Story is a trademark of The
Rowman & Littlefield Publishing Group, Inc.

Distributed by NATIONAL BOOK NETWORK

Portions of this book were previously published in *How to Rock Climb*, 6th Edition, by John Long and Bob
Gaines (FalconGuides, 2023), *Climbing Anchors*, 3rd Edition, by John Long and Bob Gaines (FalconGuides,
2013), *Climbing Anchors Field Guide*, 2nd Edition, by John Long and Bob Gaines (FalconGuides, 2014),
Toproping: Rock Climbing for the Outdoor Beginner by Bob Gaines (FalconGuides, 2020), *Advanced Rock Climbing: Mastering Sport and Trad Climbing*, by Bob Gaines (FalconGuides, 2018), and *Rappelling* by Bob Gaines
(FalconGuides, 2013).

British Library Cataloguing-in-Publication Information available

Library of Congress Cataloging-in-Publication Data available

ISBN 978-1-4930-7457-0 (paper: alk. paper)
ISBN 978-1-4930-7458-7 (electronic)

♾️™ The paper used in this publication meets the minimum requirements of American National Standard
for Information Sciences—Permanence of Paper for Printed Library Materials, ANSI/NISO Z39.48-1992.

On the Lamb *(5.9), Tuolumne Meadows, Yosemite National Park, California*

Contents

About the Authors..*vi*

Introduction..*1*

Simple Anchors

Chapter 1. Natural Anchors...*3*

Chapter 2. Nuts (aka Chocks)...*13*

    Oppositional Nuts... 19

    Micronuts 22

    Hexes 24

    Tricams 27

Chapter 3. Cams...*29*

Chapter 4. Bolts..*43*

Chapter 5. Fall Forces *51*

Chapter 6. Judging the Direction of Pull *57*

Chapter 7. Knots for Anchoring *61*

Anchor Systems

Chapter 8. Belay Anchors *71*

    STRANDS Anchors 71

    Cordelettes.. 76

    The Sliding X 90

    The Quad 96

    Composite Anchors: Cordelette, Sliding X, and Quad.................... 104

    Upward Oppositional Anchors 105

    Belay Methods 109

Chapter 9. Toprope Anchors *117*

Chapter 10. The Joshua Tree System *121*

Chapter 11. Rappel Anchors *133*

Index.. 143

About the Authors

John Long is an acclaimed rock climber and author of more than forty books, including several in Falcon's catalog. He is one of the most prolific adventure writers out there and has authored magazine articles, screenplays, documentary films, and television and movie scripts, as well as instructional rock climbing books.

Beginning in the mid-1970s with his historic one-day ascent of *The Nose* route on El Capitan, Long became a mainstay in the world of extreme sports and adventure. He and his elite group of climbers, the "Stonemasters," ushered in a new era of big-wall climbing with their epic climbs in Yosemite National Park and elsewhere. In the years that followed, John transitioned from rock climbing to international exploration, traveling around the world from the jungles of Southeast Asia to the North Pole. Some of his many achievements include the first coast-to-coast traverse of Borneo and the discovery and exploration of the world's largest river cave.

John has also built a successful television and film career, producing the *International Guinness Book of World Records* television show before moving to feature films. The Sylvester Stallone movie *Cliffhanger* is based on one of John's stories.

In recent years, John has continued to write books and articles and to work in television and film. He is also an Adidas Ambassador and frequently works with them at various events around the country.

Bob Gaines began rock climbing at Joshua Tree National Park in the 1970s. Since then he has pioneered more than 500 first ascents in the park.

Bob began his career as a professional rock climbing guide in 1983 and is an American Mountain Guides Association Certified Rock Instructor. He is the coauthor of *Rock Climbing: The AMGA Single Pitch Manual*, the textbook for the AMGA's single-pitch instructor program.

Bob has worked extensively in the film business as a climbing stunt coordinator. He has coordinated more than forty television commercials and was Sylvester Stallone's climbing instructor for the movie *Cliffhanger*. Bob doubled for William Shatner in *Star Trek V: The Final Frontier* as Captain Kirk free soloing on El Capitan in Yosemite.

Bob has worked extensively training US military special forces, including the elite US Navy SEAL Team 6, and is known for his technical expertise in anchoring and rescue techniques.

He is also the author of *Best Climbs Joshua Tree National Park*, *Best Climbs Tahquitz and Suicide Rocks*, *Toproping: Rock Climbing for the Outdoor Beginner*, *Rappelling*, and *Advanced Rock Climbing* and is coauthor of *How to Rock Climb* and *Rock Climbing: The Art of Safe Ascent* (with John Long).

Bob's other passion is fly fishing. He currently holds thirteen International Game Fish Association world records.

Introduction

Many readers would take an anchor-building seminar and later review anchor fundamentals in *Climbing Anchors*, the definitive sourcebook on anchors for all climbers in all lands. But when they ventured onto the rock and had to work strictly from memory, details were hard to recall. Toting *Climbing Anchors* to the cliffside was neither practical nor desired. This small-format print version—with its sidebars and bullet points, photos and illustrations—has proven more practical than all other options, including digital (phone) versions. Leave the *Field Guide* lying around the house, to pick up and peruse at your leisure or for taking on flights. However you might use this *Field Guide*, it was built as a companion, to take with you—out to the crags, and beyond.

Remember:

Basic Anchor-Building Facts

- "Perfect" rarely exists in real-world climbing anchors.
- No single rigging technique will work in every situation.
- Trad climbers must efficiently improvise on a handful of anchor-building techniques.
- The ability to improvise requires a thorough understanding of basic principles.
- Climbing anchors always involve compromises—the trick is to understand what you should and should not compromise at a given place on the rock.

The fine points of the systems remain works-in-progress as new materials, equipment, and refinements are introduced into the field and marketplace. Nevertheless, the material in this edition represents the combined, cutting-edge knowledge of both professional guides and leading climbers worldwide.

A bomber pine tree tied off with a cordelette. Here the cordelette has been looped around the trunk and tied with a figure-8 loop, creating redundancy in both the cord around the tree and the two loops at the master point, which the carabiners are clipped into. Simple, strong, and redundant. In all such setups, try to keep the inside angle of the cord/sling less than 90 degrees to avoid load multiplication.

Simple Anchors

CHAPTER ONE

Natural Anchors

Natural Anchors Are:

- Anything the environment provides—trees, blocks, horns of rock, etc.
- Often more secure than gear-built anchors
- Typically easy and fast to arrange
- Multidirectional (can be loaded from any direction)
- By and large environmentally friendly

When Anchoring to a Tree . . .

- The tree is living and structurally sound.
- The trunk and base are vertically aligned, not crooked like a Halloween oak.
- The tree is rooted in soil (not in sand or gravel) with no voids.
- The trunk is symmetrical at its base.

Bad. Not only is this rigging nonredundant, the sling is too short, so the carabiner is being loaded in three directions. This is known as triaxial loading.

Very bad. The sling is too short, and the single carabiner has shifted so the load is on the minor axis, straight outward on the gate.

Top left: A properly girth-hitched nylon sling

Top right: A double-length (48-inch) nylon sling tied with an overhand knot makes the sling itself redundant.

Bottom: A figure-8 follow-through knot used to tie the anchor rigging rope directly to the tree

A rigging rope tied directly to a tree using a bowline knot with a fisherman's backup. Remember, a bowline knot requires a backup knot, because it can work itself loose if the tail is too short.

Tensile Strength vs. Loop Strength

Strength ratings for cord and webbing are often given as *tensile strength* and *loop strength*. Tensile strength is tested by a straight pull on a single strand of the material with no knots, done by wrapping the material around a smooth bar (4 inches in diameter gives the most accurate test) on both ends and pulling until it breaks. Loop strength is the strength of the material tested in a loop configuration, either tied with a knot or, in the case of webbing, sewn with bartacked stitching. In general, webbing loop strength when tied with a water knot is about 80 percent of twice the tensile breaking strength, and bartacked sewn webbing loop strength is generally about 15 percent stronger than the same material tied with a water knot, depending on the quality and number of bartacks.

- Only their mass and position keep boulders and blocks in place.
- To serve as secure anchors, boulders and blocks must be sufficiently large and totally immovable.

This large block is well situated and is bomber for the direction of pull for which it is rigged. As always, appraising the integrity of a natural rock anchor involves judgment. Carefully examine for cracks in the block. And most importantly, how well is the block attached to the main rock structure? If you decide to use a detached block, how big is it: the size of your car or the size of your ice chest? Does it rest on a flat platform or a sloping shelf? As a general rule, many climbers avoid rigging anchors off detached blocks and flakes.

A monolithic but detached block. A good rule of thumb for using detached blocks is one Bob adopted from Yosemite Search and Rescue Team protocol: For a detached granite block to be used as an anchor, it must be as large as a full-size refrigerator resting lengthwise on a flat surface.

This 3-foot-diameter doorknob-shaped horn is "attached to the planet," and its unique shape allows it to be tied off in such a way as to stand even a slightly upward pull.

This beefy horn of rock is "attached to the planet," which is what you're looking for, rather than a detached formation sitting "on top of the planet." The cordelette is doubled around the horn and tied with an overhand knot, making the cord itself redundant—an extra precaution to safeguard against the cord being cut by a sharp edge.

Whatever the Rock Feature . . .

- Look out for sharp edges.
- Test the security of the feature by thumping it with the heel of your hand. Anything that wiggles or sounds hollow is suspect.
- Look for surrounding cracks.
- Tie off as close to the main wall as possible, to reduce leverage.
- Tie off with runners, slipknotting if the form is rounded.

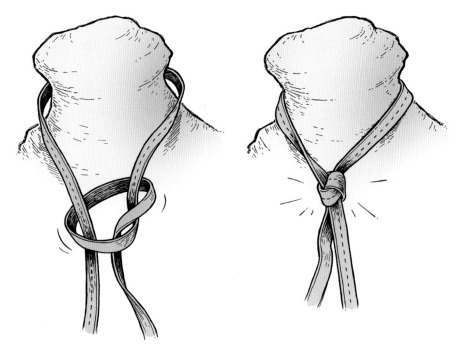

Using a slipknot to sling a horn

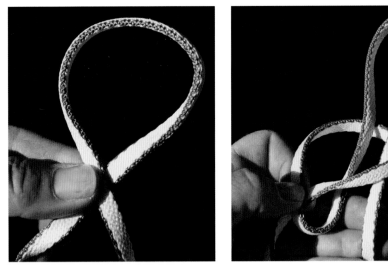

How to tie a slipknot. A slipknot can be tightened down by pulling on one strand, making it a good choice for tying off knobs of rock.

A double-length (48-inch) nylon sling girth-hitched to a horn of rock. If this were to be used for pro, the rope action through the carabiner might loosen the sling. A better setup is to choke the sling back on itself.

Although this configuration weakens the sling by 30 to 40 percent, it increases the chances of the sling staying put.

Using a sling or cord threaded through a tunnel or pocket is called a thread. This thread anchor uses a 5 mm Bluewater Titan cordelette (3,080 lb. tensile strength), doubled first, threaded through, then tied with an overhand knot, giving tremendous redundancy and quadruple strength in the cord itself. This thread is in strong granite; this same tunnel in a softer rock, like sandstone, would be much weaker and unreliable. Also, the arch of rock just above the cord appears to be partially cracked, a sign of a structural integrity deficit.

Threads like this are rare in granite but more common in limestone. Here a low-stretch rigging rope is tied with a bowline and fisherman's backup.

A chockstone tied off with a girth-hitched sling. This chockstone, while good for a straight-down pull, has surface contact only at the top left and looks like it could pivot free if any outward or upward force is applied.

CHAPTER TWO

Nuts (aka Chocks)

Basic Rules of Placing a Good Nut

- The nut has to be bigger—if only a bit—than the section of crack below where it is lodged.
- Slot the nut that most closely corresponds to the geometry of the crack.
- Whenever possible, set the nut where the crack not only pinches off in the downward direction but also in the outward direction.
- Orient the nut so the cable or sling points in the expected direction of pull/loading.
- Try to get the majority of the nut set against the rock, maximizing the amount of surface contact.
- Avoid endwise placements if possible, as they tend to be less secure.
- If you have a choice, go with the bigger nut, as it is generally more secure, with more surface area contacting the rock.
- Make sure the placement is well seated, with no movement or rattle when weighted by hand.

Use the SOS Acronym to Assess a Nut Placement

S **Structural integrity** of the rock itself. Look for straight-in cracks in massive rock; avoid flakes, blocks, and rotten cracks.

O **Orientation.** Place the nut with the anticipated direction of pull in mind. It may hold a ton in one direction but be easily dislodged with a tug in the opposite direction.

S **Surface Contact.** Always strive for maximum flushness between the faces of the chock and the rock.

Both sides of this Stopper have great surface contact, and the constriction of the crack corresponds with the shape of the taper. Grade: A.

Like a man too big for his trousers, this nut simply doesn't fit. It probably will hold body weight, but not much more. Grade: D-.

A bomber endwise placement of a size 12 Stopper. Maximum flush surface contact, plus a lip on the crack to prevent outward pull from dislodging it, earns this placement an A+. For larger Stoppers (size 10, 11, 12, and 13), the strength rating of the endwise placement equals the strength of the narrower configuration (10k N or 2,248 lb.).

This Wild Country Rock has excellent surface contact on its left side but hardly any on its right side. This placement is not bomber—maybe good enough to hang off, but if this nut was all that was keeping you from hitting the deck, you'd best quickly look for other placements. Grade: D-.

Stopper in a bottleneck placement. There is simply no way that in a downward pull the nut could be pulled through the bottleneck— something would have to give, either the rock itself or the nut or wire cable breaking. Grade: A-.

This Stopper placement is in a good bottleneck and would easily hold a straight downward force, but what makes it borderline marginal is its lack of surface contact on the left side, making it susceptible to being yanked with even nominal outward force. If this is all you've got, set it as well as you can with a downward jerk, then test it with an outward tug and see what happens, taking care not to hit yourself in the face or teeth if the nut suddenly pops. Grade: C+.

A solid endwise Stopper placement: flush surface contact and a lip to the crack to prevent any outward force from dislodging the placement. Grade: A.

This endwise placement is in a slight but shallow bottleneck. The trapezoidal shape of the nut fits the shallow slot. If well set, this nut earns a B-.

The Stopper placement is flush in this endwise configuration, but how strong is that nubbin of rock on the right wall of the crack? Probably strong enough to hang off, but maybe not strong enough to hold a leader on a 30-foot ripper. Believe it: The principal cause of pro placement failure is rock failure. Protection devices seldom break, but they often rip out, meaning security, not strength, is generally the main issue. Grade: D+.

Even though the crack is flared, this offset nut (meaning one edge is wider than the other) has great surface contact and fits the shape of the crack in both dimensions. Grade: A.

Both the ball nut and removable bolt are based upon this concept (opposition). While this configuration ("stacked" Stoppers) will work, it is very rarely used. In this case these two Stoppers mate together rather well, and both have flush contact with each other and the wall of the crack. Grade: B-.

Horizontal placements (relatively rare) like this require a crack that is wider here and narrower just left or right. Wiggle the nut into the wider section, then slide it sideways into a narrower constriction. Such nuts can easily snag during cleaning. Back the placement out the way it was installed. Grade B+.

This Wild Country Rock placement has three points of contact, which locks in the placement, although more surface contact is preferable. Grade: C+.

While the right side lacks surface contact, this Wild Country Rock is so keyed into a bottleneck there's no way, in a straight, downward pull, that the nut could pull through the constriction. Grade: B-.

Oppositional Nuts

Nuts in opposition, tied together with a clove hitch on a sling, can help solve the direction-of-pull dilemma, especially when a spring loaded camming device (SLCD) placement is not available. (See the Knots for Anchoring chapter for a detailed description of how to tie a clove hitch.) This configuration will also work for nuts opposed in a horizontal crack.

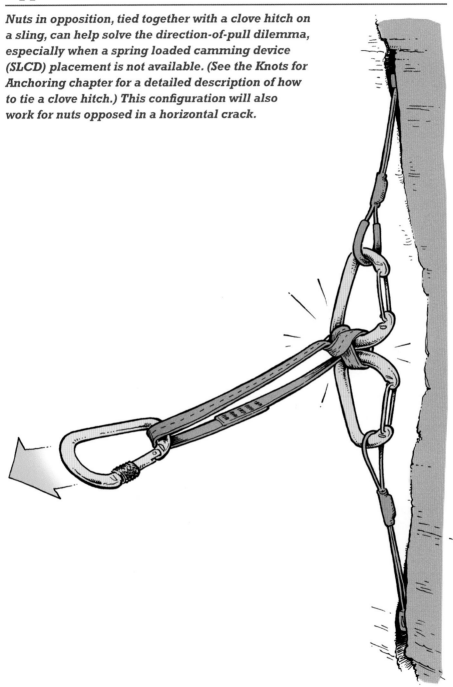

Here is what you'll commonly encounter when rigging oppositional nuts: two placements, slightly spaced apart, tied off with two separate clove hitches.

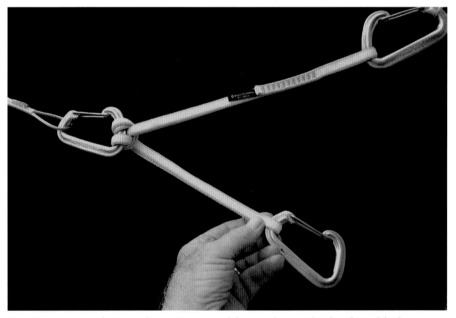

Another way to rig two pieces in opposition, using a single clove hitch.

1. Another method to tension oppositional pieces together. This method is easier to rig with one hand if you're on the lead, in a spot where you can't let go with both hands. Start by clipping the sling into one carabiner, then run the sling through the other carabiner.

3. Take the sling through the carabiner.

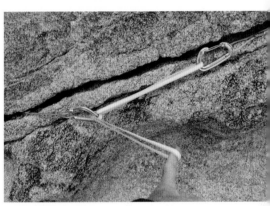

4. Tighten it.

2. Thread the sling between the two strands of the sling, between the carabiners.

5. Clip in and you're good to go.

Micronuts

Tips for Using Micronuts

- The surface area contact of every micro is quite small. Only ideal placements are secure.

- Micros are usually reliable only in dense rock (granite, limestone, etc.)

- Lateral forces easily pivot micros out of cracks; always slot the micro directly in the line of pull. This also prevents tweaking the cable.

- For lead pro, extend all micro placements with quickdraws. Rope drag can easily displace the micro.

- Avoid placements where the wire is running over an edge.

- Avoid jerking the micro too hard, either when setting or removing it, lest you prematurely bend, weaken, or even break the wire.

This #6 Micro Stopper has a breaking strength of 8 kN (1,789 lb.) Although set in a bottleneck, this placement lacks surface contact on its right side and, because of the stiff wire, is susceptible to being plucked out by an outward force. The next smaller size would fit better. When I'm (BG) leading, I carry groups of small nuts on an oval carabiner, about a half-dozen of similar size per carabiner, and use them like a set of keys. If one doesn't fit, I'll go to the next size, keeping them all on the carabiner. Once I find my placement, I'll unclip the carabiner and put a quickdraw on the placement. Grade for this placement: D.

This Black Diamond Micro Stopper has great surface contact on the left side—almost 100 percent flush—which is what you're looking for. The right side is also nearly flush, plus the nut simply fits the slot. To secure truly bomber placements, scan the crack for the "V-slot" configuration and place the nut that best fits the slot. Remember to set the placement with several downward tugs and give it a test by yanking slightly out and up. A poorly seated nut may hold a ton with a straight, downward load but may be yanked up and out with a minimal force (like rope drag). Review the breaking strengths of the nuts you buy, and take this into consideration when building your anchor. This number 3 Micro Stopper has a breaking strength of 5 kN (1,123 lb.), compared to a number 6 Stopper of 10 kN (2,248 lb.). Grade for this placement: B.

Because of micros' boxy shape, near parallel-sided cracks often afford the best placements. Careful placement is essential, because the relative differences between a good and bad micro placement are small indeed. While it is tempting to slot the nut deep in the crack, it's usually better to keep it where you can visually assess the placement. Here the micro shows good, flush surface contact on both sides of the crack in this endwise placement. Grade: B+.

Hexes

Top left: This Hex placement, set in a solid, straight-in crack, has near-perfect flushness on both faces of the nut. Loading the nut's cable will activate the camming action of the Hex. Grade: A+.

Top right: This is what to look for: great surface contact on both sides, with the curve of the nut form-fitting the slot in the rock. Bomber! Grade: A.

Bottom: Bomber. Great surface contact. A load on this nut would create a camming effect to further key it into the crack. Grade: A+.

You couldn't hang your hat on this dud—a poor endwise placement. The right side is flush against the wall of the crack, but look at the left side! Minimal surface contact. This nut simply does not correspond to the geometry of the crack and would likely fail if loaded. Grade: F.

A picture-perfect endwise placement—flush contact on both ends, well seated, and bomber. Set it well and you're good to go. A+.

This Black Diamond Hex is well seated in a pocket in the crack, with excellent surface contact on both faces of the chock. When a load is applied, the camming action will kick in, further wedging it in the crack. Placements such as this are great for a downward pull, but they must be well set to safeguard against any outward force. If using it as a piece of pro for leading, a quickdraw or sling will help safeguard against this possibility.

Close inspection of this Hex placement reveals a lack of flush surface contact on the right side and on the inside of the Hex. Also, the rock microstructure is large grained and therefore potentially weak. This could be a problem since the crack really opens up below the nut. Ideally you want the crack narrower below any nut placement so the nut has nowhere to go even if the grainy surface of the rock fails.

Tricams

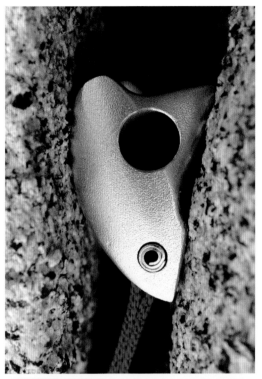

A tricam placed in the passive mode as a chock. Grade: A-.

A tricam in camming position. Grade: A.

Not good. This tricam is set in camming mode with the point resting on a crystal, meaning it's unlikely to withstand much sideways rope wiggle, and it might fall out of the crack under even slight outward pressure. Grade: D-.

CHAPTER THREE

Cams

The Basic Essentials of Placing Spring-Loaded Camming Devices (SLCDs)

- Always align the unit with the stem pointing in the anticipated direction of pull.

- To keep the unit from "walking" because of rope drag during a lead, clip a quickdraw into the sewn sling of the unit.

- Try to place the unit near the outside edge of the crack, where you can eyeball the cam lobes to determine their position. This also makes it easier to reach the trigger to clean the device.

- Strive for the ideal placement, with the cams deployed/retracted in the most uniformly parallel section of the crack, so the cams cannot open if the unit walks a bit. Metolius puts color-coded dots on the cams to help with lobe positioning, but with others you'll have to eyeball it. Read and follow the manufacturer's recommendations for cam deployment.

- Use a larger device over a smaller one, but unless you are absolutely desperate, never force too big a unit into too small a hole. Once the cams are rolled to minimum width, removal, if even possible, is grievous.

- Never trust a placement where the cams are nearly "tipped" (the cam lobes almost fully deployed). In such a position there is little room for further expansion, and stability is poor.

- Never place a rigid-stemmed unit so the stem is over a lip. A fall can either bend or break the unit. SLCD manufacturer Wild Country recommends using the "Gunk's tie off" for horizontal placements, which is a pre-tied loop of high-tensile, 5.5 mm diameter cord threaded through the hole closest to the cam head. Clipping in to this loop prevents torque on the rigid stem.

- Take some time to experiment with marginal placements on the ground. Clip a sling into the SLCD and apply body weight to discover just how far you can trust it. But remember—body weight testing is far milder than a lead fall!

Assessing SLCD Placements

When assessing a camming device placement, the key elements are:

1. Rock Structure. Evaluate both macro- and microstructural integrity.

2. Placement in parallel-sided cracks.

3. Orientation—placed in the direction of pull.

4. Range of Retraction (to manufacturer's guidelines—e.g., 50–90 percent for Camalots).

5. Test for walking. Tug on the placement and wiggle it slightly; beware of cracks that widen above and below the placement.

A useful acronym for all cam placements is **SPORT**:

    S Structural integrity of the rock
    P Placement in parallel-sided crack
    O Orientation (direction of pull)
    R Range of retraction
    T Test for walking

This placement looks good, but how strong is that flake forming the crack's right side? Dubious. Grade: F.

Camalot placed for lead protection. The crack and the placement look good, but how strong is the flake? In general, avoid flakes and seek straight-in cracks that bisect the plane of the rock face at a 90-degree angle.

The inside cams of this Black Diamond Camalot are deployed beyond the acceptable range. Given the widening crack above the device, any to-and-fro action will "walk" the placement into the wider section. If loaded, such a placement would likely fail. Grade: D-.

This Wild Country Friend is retracted tight and placed in the most parallel-sided section of this crack. The crack is slightly flared, angling slightly outward (first red flag), and widening below the device (second red flag). Grade: C-.

All the cams are in the recommended ideal range (50–90 percent retraction), and the placement is in a parallel-sided, rock-solid crack. When placing Camalots strive for retraction at 50 percent (and tighter), when the cam lobes describe a 45-degree angle relative to the vertical axis (the direction on the stem), or when the bases of the cams form a 90-degree angle relative to each other. Grade: A.

A near ideal placement of a Wild Country Friend. With double-axle design camming devices, strive for a placement where the bottom tips of the camming lobes all line up, which is what we have here, about 80 percent retracted. Grade: A-.

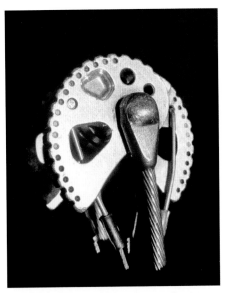

The Metolius company was first to adopt a color-coding system that helps us evaluate cam placements. Green is within the recommended range. Yellow means caution—you're slightly out of optimal range. Red means danger—you're making a potentially bad placement.

Metolius cams' color-coded dots assist in assessing your placement. Green is the recommended range (75–100 percent retracted). Yellow means caution; you're slightly out of optimal range—the next larger size cam offers a better fit. Red means danger; you're making a bad (too-open) placement. The grade for this Metolius Master Cam placement: A.

Metolius recommends that in a horizontal crack, the outside cams should be placed on the bottom of the crack for maximum stability. Grade for this placement: A.

This Metolius Power Cam is right on the edge of the green. Remember, Metolius recommends their cams be placed in the tighter (75–100 percent retracted) range. Grade: A-.

Too tight. This Camalot is around 90 percent retracted. Any tighter, and it may be difficult, or impossible, to remove. There is loss of holding power in the last 10 percent (90–100 percent retracted on a Camalot).

The two cam lobes on the right side of the crack are outside the acceptable range for a Camalot (too wide). Also, each set of cam lobes (inside and outside) is not symmetrically retracted. The cam lobes are barely retracted and nowhere near the recommended range. The piece can easily walk and fail completely. Grade: F.

This Metolius Power Cam is set in a pocket. This lends stability to the placement, even though it is borderline on the red range-finder dots, signifying a marginal placement. The next larger size cam would fit this crack much better. Grade: C-.

While open slightly beyond the optimal range of retraction, this Camalot should have good holding power as a pro placement. Since the crack has a fairly uniform width, there should be minimal walking with any to-and-fro action of the rope—but attach a sling or quickdraw to make sure. The next larger size Camalot would provide a nicer, tighter fit. Grade: C+.

Although Camalots work in slightly flaring cracks, a parallel-sided crack is our target. Here, even though the crack is flared and the inside cams are retracted tighter than the outside ones, all four cams have good surface contact and are in the acceptable range of retraction. Grade: C-.

The crack is way too flared for this Metolius Power Cam. The cam on the right side has poor surface contact with the rock. Grade: F.

Cam placement in a horizontal crack. A leader fall may bend and tweak the flexible cable stem, which will nevertheless save the day.

The placement itself looks good, but the rock structure is questionable. How strong is that chunk of rock forming the right side of the crack? If the cam should sustain a high load, would the rock break away? Maybe not in sound granite like this, but in sandstone, say, it likely would. Best not to test it. Remember, the most important thing to consider when placing cams is the structural integrity of the rock. Grade: D-.

Here the rock is solid and the placement bomber, but in a leader fall, the carabiner would be loaded over an edge, potentially opening the gate. With the gate open, a carabiner loses two-thirds of its strength—something we never wish to test in a leader fall. An easy solution is to extend the placement with a basketed sling (right photo), clipping in the carabiner well below the edge.

Two pieces combined with a basketed sling = no carabiner loaded over the edge.

The same crack with two different placements. In the left-hand photo the right (outside) cam is too close to the edge of the crack. By flipping the cam around (right-hand photo), the outside cam is now on the left wall, and the inside cam (now on the right wall) is deeper in the crack. Since the inside and outside sets of cams are offset, flipping the camming device one way or the other can often render a better placement, particularly in shallow cracks in corners.

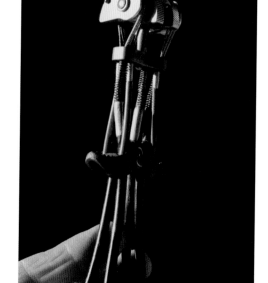

The unique Totem Cam, manufactured in Spain, has become popular in recent years.

Totem Cam with the cams about 50 percent retracted. Totem's manufacturer recommends: "It is best for the cam lobes to work at half their expansion range, i.e., when they are between 50% and 90% closed." With any new cam you buy, check the manufacturer's guidelines and instructions for use. Here the cam, with rope action, could wiggle up into the slightly wider section of the crack, and open wider (albeit just barely) than the recommended range. Grade: B-.

Here the Totem Cam is placed just above a flaring crack. The manufacturer warns: "Ensure that all the cam lobes make good contact against the rock, and that the crack beneath the contact point does not open." Grade: D.

This Totem Cam placement disregards the manufacturer's specific warning: "Do not use the Totem Cam with the lobes near to fully open. Any movement in the rope can change the position of the unit, which could fail. Use a larger Totem Cam." Grade: F.

In addition to parallel-sided cracks, Camalots also work well in pods or pockets, as shown here. Make sure the cams are in the recommended deployment range. Grade: A-.

Camalot in a horizontal slot. The placement is in a slight pocket, with the cams retracted over 50 percent, in good symmetry and with excellent surface contact. Grade: A-.

This Camalot violates a rule stated in the Black Diamond literature under "Bad Placements": "Never place a unit so that the cams are offset (e.g., with two cams extended and with two cams retracted). It may not hold a fall." Also, the left outer cam is dangerously close to the edge of the crack. Grade: F.

This placement has problems. The two outermost cams are unequally retracted. Worse yet, the crack is too flared (especially the right wall) to achieve a reliable placement. Lastly, the rock is grainy. Grade: F.

Short Course on Placing Pro

- Set your gear in solid stone.

- Use the right-sized gear for a given placement.

- Seek parallel-sided cracks for cams, "V-shaped" constrictions for nuts.

- Go for the "match fit," where the nut achieves maximum surface contact (sets flush) against the walls of the crack.

- Try to avoid shallow and/or flared placements, or those set too deep in the crack.

- An ideal placement is secure once set and straightforward to clean (remove).

About Setting Safe Protection—
Passive or Active:

- No rock-climbing anchor is 100 percent reliable. Appropriate backups are essential for secure climbing.

- Before setting a nut or cam, first look for a strong, quick placement, considering possible directions of loading.

- Try to slot passive nuts in constrictions where, to ever pull through, the nut would be reduced to something as thin as beer can aluminum.

- Always visually inspect the placement. If the passive placement seems loose, set it with a tug.

- Nuts and cams pull out under frighteningly small loads when set in poor rock.

- Avoid setting anchors behind shaky flakes or loose blocks; you run the risk of pulling these down if you peel off.

- Most passive nuts can be positioned in several attitudes. Familiarize yourself with the primary, or preferred, position and go with that whenever possible. It is usually more stable.

- Be especially careful not to dislodge the piece with your body (often a foot as you climb past), rack, or rope after you have placed it.

- If you have never used a certain type of gear, practice placing it on the ground (extensively) before thumbing it into a seam and casting off for a lieback.

- The majority of your primary placements will be cams. Master their use.

- Inspect your gear frequently. Retire hardware if you observe cracks or other defects in the metal, or if the cable becomes kinked.

CHAPTER FOUR

Bolts

Top: The ³⁄₈-inch diameter hex-head Powers "Power Bolt" expansion bolt with a stainless-steel hanger has become somewhat of a minimum standard for climbing anchor bolts. These were formerly known as "Rawl bolts," but the Rawl brand was acquired by the Powers Company. In good granite the ³⁄₈-inch diameter Power Bolt is rated at over 7,000 pounds shear strength, with a pullout strength of roughly 5,000 pounds. If you're installing bolts, use stainless-steel bolts and match them with stainless-steel hangers (such as the Petzl hanger shown here) to prevent galvanic corrosion, which is a reaction between two different types of metal. Although stainless bolts are far more expensive than carbon steel bolts, they'll last decades longer.

Bottom: Another commonly used bolt is the ³⁄₈-inch wedge bolt.

A properly installed wedge bolt. In a proper installation, the hanger should be tight to the rock and the threaded tip of the bolt should protrude a minimum of 3 mm above the nut, but no more than 6 mm.

On the left is a contraction bolt (³/₈-inch diameter Powers Drive, formerly known as a Rawl Drive), and on the right is the ³/₈-inch diameter Power Bolt, both manufactured by the Powers Company. Contraction bolts can be easily identified by their mushroom head and are unreliable in soft rock (like sandstone), since they rely on the rock itself to compress the split shaft. In soft rock the hole tolerance is often too big, especially if drilled by hand. Even if a perfect hole is drilled with a rotary-hammer power drill, the bolt can groove its way into the soft rock, often without contracting the split shaft enough to produce the tension required for good holding power. In fine-grained granite with a proper-size hole, the shaft will contract, and the ³/₈-inch and ⁵/₁₆-inch diameter sizes are reliable in good, solid rock. The ¼-inch size is usually a relic from the past and must be used with caution.

Buttonhead contraction bolts (left to right): $^3/_8$*-,* $^5/_{16}$*-, and* $^1/_4$ *-inch sizes*

Learn the difference between these two hangers, one good, one very bad, both manufactured by the SMC Company and stamped "SMC" on the hanger. These are relics of the past, but you might come across this type of hanger on an old trad route. The hanger on the left is the infamous SMC "death hanger," a moniker that stuck after several such hangers failed under body weight (possibly due to a stress corrosion problem) on Yosemite's Middle Cathedral Rock. The "bad" SMC hangers are identifiable by a distinctive corrosive discoloration—a yellowish or bronze tint—whereas the "good" SMC hangers (on the right), made from stainless steel, show no signs of corrosion or rust and appear silvery bright, even after 30 years of exposure to the elements. Another noticeable difference is the thickness of the hangers—the "bad" hangers roughly the thickness of a dime, and the "good" hangers roughly the thickness of a quarter. The crucial identifying feature is: on the "bad" hanger, the letters "SMC" are stamped horizontally; on the "good" hanger, "SMC" is stamped vertically. The "good" SMC hangers are reliable, even after 30 years, but clip the SMC "death hangers" at your peril.

Another hanger to watch out for is the infamous "Leeper hanger." Over 9,000 made it into circulation, and they've all been recalled by the manufacturer due to stress corrosion problems in the chrome moly steel. The good news is that they're easy to identify, due to their odd geometric shape and rusty condition.

This ⅜-inch diameter bolt, placed in the 1970s at Suicide Rock, is badly corroded with a Leeper hanger to match. Not to be trusted.

An old threaded Rawl Drive bolt. A problem with this design is that the outward holding power is only as strong as the threads holding the nut in place. This flaw was responsible for a death in Yosemite on a route on Glacier Point Apron named Anchors Away. If you come across one of these ticking time bombs, make sure the nut is screwed down as far as it will go, and use it with caution.

Behold the woeful "spinner." This buttonhead bolt protrudes from the hole, and the hanger is not flush against the rock. The hole was not drilled deep enough, and when hammered in, the shaft bottomed out in the back of the hole, preventing the head of the bolt from pinning the hanger flush against the rock.

A relic from the old days, this ¼-inch Rawl Drive buttonhead still looks good after 25 years; the "good" SMC stainless-steel hanger shows no signs of corrosion. In trad climbing areas most aging ¼-inch bolts have been replaced, but you'll still find some on more obscure climbs, stuck in the stone like slow-ticking time bombs. In fine-grained, iron-hard granite, one of these contraction bolts might hold 2,000 pounds. In anything less than perfect rock, old Rawl buttonheads should never be trusted. Here the placement looks acceptable: The bolt is perpendicular to the plane of the rock face, and the head of the bolt and hanger is flush to the rock. What can't be judged by visual inspection is the length of the bolt. These ¼-inch buttonheads come in lengths ranging from ¾ inch to 1½ inches. Bob has replaced dozens of ¼-inch bolts over the years. Many were removed simply by putting a claw hammer behind the hanger and prying outward, with about the same force required as pulling a nail from a piece of particleboard.

A $^5/_{16}$-inch buttonhead contraction bolt with a "good" SMC hanger. In a sound placement in solid granite, when new these bolts were rated at more than 4,000 pounds shear strength. But since they're made of carbon steel, they've corroded over time and are now considered suspect.

A well-placed, $^3/_8$-inch stainless Power Bolt matched with a stainless-steel hanger. Good to go.

Metolius sells hangers in various colors to match the color of the rock. This is important in areas where bolting is controversial, and it reduces visual pollution for non-climbers from bright, shiny hangers. Many climbers go one step further and custom paint the hangers before installation to blend into the rock.

What to Do with That Bolt . . .

There is no reliable method to test in situ bolts but plenty of reasons to want to. Here are some suggestions:

- Always consider a ¼-inch bolt suspect. They have not been placed as anchors for decades, though some are still found on older, "legacy" routes.

- Make sure the bolt hanger is flush to the wall and not a "spinner," where the hanger spins freely on the stud. A spinner indicates the hole was drilled too shallow for the bolt stud or that the stud has crept out from the hole, which happens with contraction bolts. With a Hex-head expansion bolt, you can try tightening it with a wrench, but most likely the bolt has a problem and needs to be replaced.

- Keep an eye out for cratering, which occurs in brittle or extremely hard rock and is usually the result of sloppy drilling, which forms a chipped-away crater around the hole. Cratering can greatly reduce the bolt's purchase because the rock surrounding the shank is damaged or missing.

- Check the hanger for cracks.

- For bolts with threaded ends, make sure the nut is snug and the threads are in good shape. If the bolt is a buttonhead, or looks like a machine bolt, again make sure it is snugly set and free of fatigue cracks.

- If the bolt is clearly bent or looks to be set in an oblique hole, beware!

- Discoloration is natural enough, but excessive rust denotes a "coffin nail." Use common sense. If the bolt looks funky, do not trust it. And always back up bolts (that do not meet the modern standard) with a nut or cam, if possible. A perfect bolt is nearly impossible to pull out, but scads of bolts out there are less than perfect.

CHAPTER FIVE

Fall Forces

Forces Facts

- The top piece always absorbs the greatest force during a fall; therefore, the top piece is the most important component in the entire belay chain—be it a point of protection (ideal), or the belay anchor itself (worst case).

- A well-engineered belay, combined with good belaying technique, limits loading on the topmost piece of protection.

- The most critical time is when a leader is first leaving the belay and has yet to place the first piece of protection (the Jesus Nut).

- The belay anchor is not completed, and the roped safety system is not truly on-line, till a secure Jesus Nut is placed.

The Jesus Nut

Jesus Nut is a term made infamous by helicopter mechanics during the Vietnam War. The then-ubiquitous Bell "Huey" Iroquois helicopter had one and only one giant, stainless-steel nut (the Jesus Nut) that screwed onto the top of the main rotor mast, keeping the main rotor blades attached to the copter. As the saying went, "If it fails, the next person you see will be Jesus."

Rock climbing needed a simple, dedicated term to indicate the critical first placement off the belay anchor, ergo the **Jesus Nut,** which might be a piton or a bolt, a cam or a sling around a horn, etc.

$$\textbf{FALL FACTOR} = \frac{\text{length of fall}}{\text{length of rope between belayer and climber}}$$

Calculating the fall factor

This climber is running the lead rope through the top piece in the anchor system as he takes off on lead. If he should fall, his full weight will come onto this piece, not the belayer, eliminating the possibility of a factor-2 fall, although unless the belayer is well braced for a pull directly toward this piece, she will get slammed into the wall. The best option is for the leader to place a bomber piece of protection as soon as possible, independent of the belay anchor, probably from his current stance, where the crack looks willing to accept a good piece.

Belaying the leader on a multipitch climb. Here the stance is well managed: The belayer has butterflied the rope across the tie-in rope so it feeds out easily during the lead. The yellow cordelette equalizes three anchor placements, and the leader's rope is clipped into the master point to protect a short traverse at the beginning of the pitch. If the leader falls, all the pieces in the anchor, not just one, come into play, but the belayer better be well braced so they don't get sucked into the carabiner where the leader's rope is clipped.

Facing page: Hanging belay at Red Rocks, Nevada. Here, Mike Moretti pays out the leader's rope, clipped to the right bolt of a two-bolt anchor with a locking carabiner, eliminating a factor-2 fall potential. Mike has attached himself to the master point with a clove hitch and braced himself for an upward pull if the leader were to fall on this traverse up and right from the anchor. He's adjusted his stance to create a little distance between his belay device and the first point the leader's rope is clipped into. His rope is well managed—butterfly-looped across his tie-in strand.

Climbers on Crimson Cringe in Yosemite. The sooner the leader can get that first bomber piece in (the "Jesus Nut") the better, so as to avoid the dreaded factor-2 fall right onto the belayer's device—a hard catch for the belayer. In this case the leader has done just that, with the first piece placed right above the anchor. If the leader clips the rope into the highest piece of the anchor, and that piece sustains a fall, the belayer will most likely get pulled hard and slammed in that direction.

CHAPTER SIX

Judging the Direction of Pull

Direction of Pull

- Every fall generates a dynamic force that will pull on the roped safety system from a specific direction or directions.

- The direction of pull is described by a direct line between the belayer and the first piece of pro (when belaying a leader) or the last piece of pro (when belaying a follower) through which the rope runs.

- Lead protection and belay anchors must sustain loading from every direction of pull that is possible on a specific pitch.

- To accurately judge the direction of pull, you must know where the route goes.

- When the direction of pull is uncertain, a multidirectional belay anchor is required.

- When a swinging fall directly onto protection or onto the belay anchor is possible, the pro and the belay anchor must be built to sustain loading across the full arc of the swing.

- Knowing the direction of pull is to a climber what knowing the direction of a possible ambush is to a foot soldier: essential for survival.

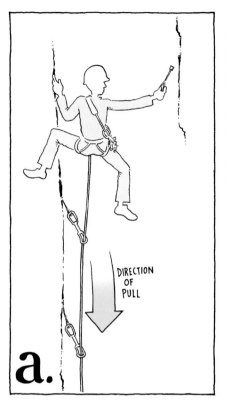

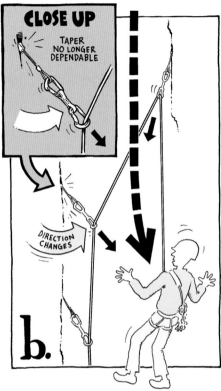

The direction of pull on protection changes with the next placement. In Figure A, the falling climber will impact the protection straight down.

Figure B shows how a fall on protection placed higher and out of a direct line with pieces below will change the direction of pull. Note that the falling climber will not pull straight down on the top piece because of the placement of the previous nut.

Straight Line

The leader's goal is for the rope to run in a relatively straight line by judicious use of quickdraws and slings, eliminating a conflagration of varying directions of pull on all the pieces in the system. At any angle created by a zigzagging rope through various pieces, if the leader falls, the resulting direction of pull will bisect every angle created.

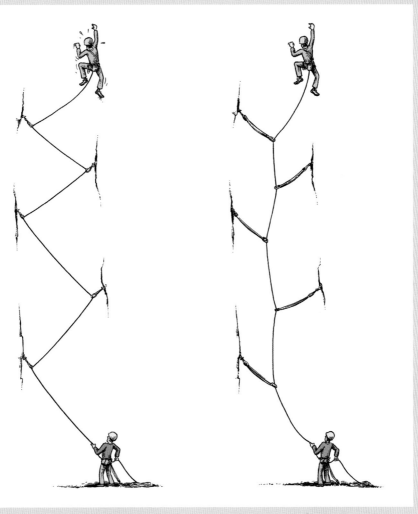

Not using runners. If the leader were to fall at this point, the direction of pull at each piece (except for the top piece), rather than straight down, would be a sideways force, bisecting each angle that has been created in the rope.

Using runners correctly. Your goal as a leader is for the rope to run in as straight a line as possible.

The leader led this Joshua Tree slab pitch by A) clipping several bolts,
B) placing a piece in the horizontal crack, C) then traversing right to the
belay ledge. Should the second (follower) fall, the direction of pull—from
the belay—will be to where the rope is clipped into the last piece in the
horizontal crack. The direction of force at that piece will bisect the angle
created in the rope system.

CHAPTER SEVEN

Knots for Anchoring

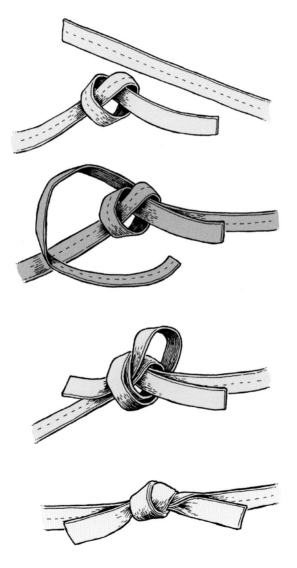

Tying the water knot (aka ring bend)

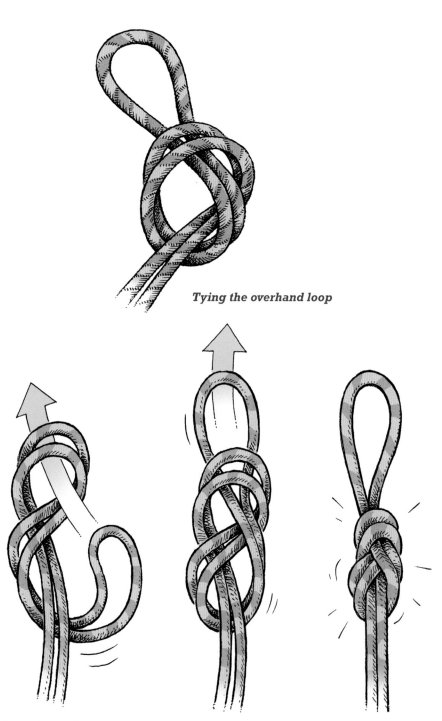

Tying the overhand loop

Tying a figure-8 loop

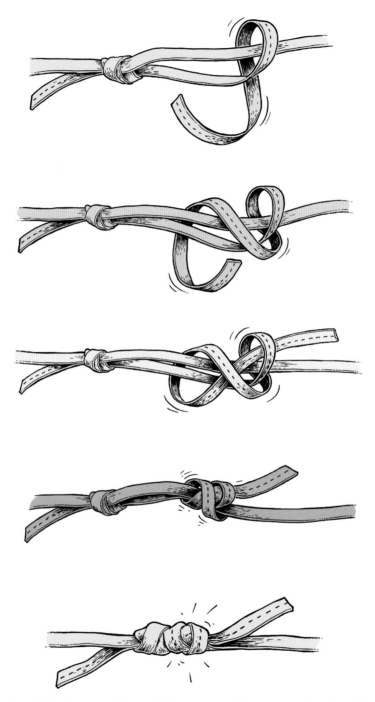

Tying a double fisherman's knot. Add one more loop around each end to make a triple fisherman's knot.

Tying a clove hitch. The load strand should be the strand closest to the spine of the carabiner.

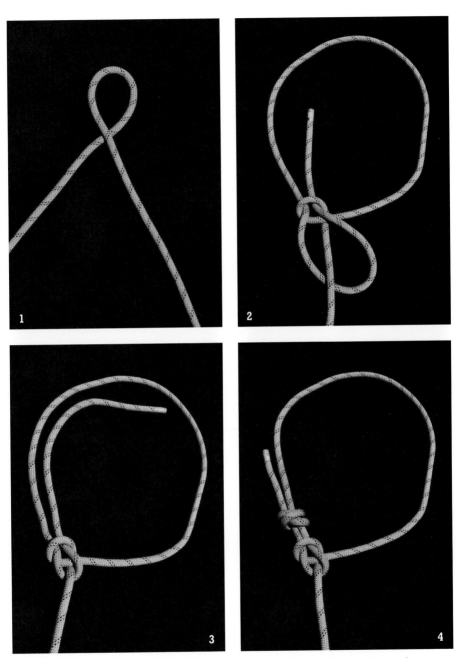

Tying a bowline. The bowline should always be tied with a backup, shown here with half a double fisherman's for the backup knot (photo 4).

The double-loop bowline (aka bowline-on-a-bight) is useful for anchoring with the rope to a two-point anchor system, such as two bolts at a hanging belay. It can also be used with a rigging rope to connect two components in a larger anchor system. Back it up with half a double fisherman's knot (photo 5).

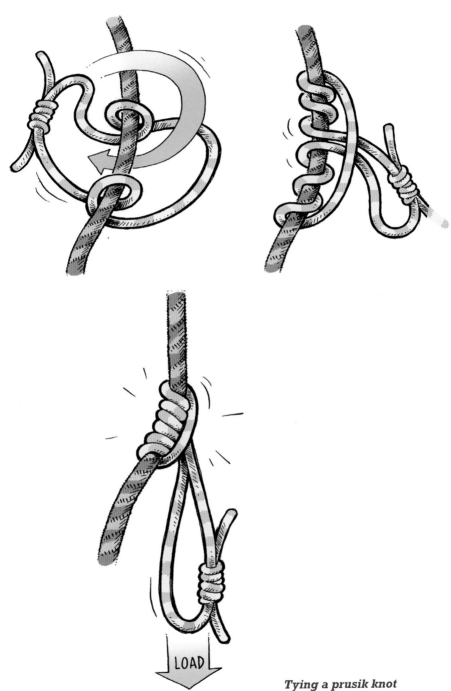

Tying a prusik knot

1. *Tying a double-loop figure-8. Take a bight of rope and cross it back over itself, forming a loop.*

3. *To finish, take the loop at the very end of the bight and fold it down and around the entire knot you've just formed.*

2. *Take two strands of the bight and wrap them around the standing part, then poke them through the loop.*

The double-loop figure-8 is a great knot to use to tie off to two anchor points. You can manipulate the knot by loosening one strand and feeding it through the body of the knot, shortening one loop, which makes the other loop longer.

Tying a Munter Hitch

1. *Grasp a single strand of rope with both hands, with thumbs pointing toward each other.*

2. *Cross the right-hand strand on top of the left-hand strand, hold the two strands where they cross with your left thumb and forefinger, then slide your right hand down about 6 inches.*

3. *Now bring the right strand up and behind the loop.*

4. *Clip a locking carabiner where the forefinger is shown here, below the top two strands.*

Tying a Munter hitch on a carabiner

Anchor Systems

CHAPTER EIGHT

Belay Anchors

STRANDS Anchors

Cliff Notes on Redundancy

- Redundancy credo: Never trust a single piece of gear.
- Proper redundancy ensures that if any one component fails, the anchor will not automatically fail.
- Redundancy asks that anchor systems be constructed of multiple components—from the primary placements to the slings and carabiners used for connecting placements.
- According to NASA, doubling-up (making redundant) components within any system greatly increases reliability over single component setups. Tripling slightly increases reliability over doubled setups. Quadrupling makes practically no difference.
- In real-world climbing you sometimes cannot make redundant every facet of the system, but there is every reason to try.
- A fail-safe anchor, not redundancy per se, is the ultimate goal, and redundancy is only one important tool to achieve that goal.

 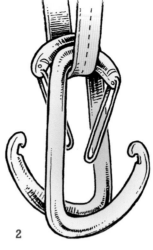

Doubled carabiners should always have the gates opposed and reversed. Locking carabiners would provide even more security.

1. *The wrong way.* Even if one of the carabiners is flipped over so the gates are on opposite sides, the gates are still not technically opposed.

2. *The right way.* Even if one of the carabiners flipped over and the gates were on the same side, the direction they open is still in opposition.

Two oval carabiners with the gates properly opposed and reversed

Two pear-shaped locking carabiners with the gates opposed and reversed at a toprope master point

The STRANDS Principle

S Solid
T Timely
R Redundancy
A Angles
N No Extension
D Distributes Load
S Simple

- **Solid** refers to the structural integrity of the rock, which we evaluate from macro to micro. Solid also refers to the security of the placement itself. Have you placed the piece as it was designed to be placed? Solid placements in solid rock. That's what solid means, and it remains the foundation of all anchors all the time.

- **Timely** refers to our efficiency in constructing an anchor. This is critical on long, multipitch routes where too much time spent building anchors can mean the difference between topping out at dusk and an unplanned bivy on the cliff.

- **Redundant** means there is no place in the anchor system where you rely on a single piece of gear, be it a strand of cord, sling, or carabiner. There is always a backup. For bolt anchors, the minimum is two bolts, preferably ⅜-inch diameter. For gear anchors, the minimum number (and the industry standard for guides) is three cams and/or nuts. If the rock quality is questionable, using two different rock features (e.g., two different crack systems) adds redundancy.

- **Angles** addresses the load multiplication that occurs when the outside arms of a rigging system (which form a V) are spread too far apart. If you keep the "V angle" under 60 degrees, you split the load roughly 50/50. Rule of thumb: The angle between the arms in any belay anchor should never exceed 90 degrees—less, if at all possible (see illustration on page 78).

- **No Extension** means that if any one piece in the anchor system fails, no significant amount of slack will develop before the load abruptly shifts to the remaining pieces (often called "shock loading," mostly a muddied term). The rule of thumb is to limit any possible extension in your anchor system to no more than half the length of a single (24-inch) sling—12 inches.

- **Distributes Load** means that when the master point is loaded, the loading is distributed among the various components (primary placements) of the anchor. "Distributed" has come to replace "equalized," which in years past suggested that the load was evenly spread across placements in the anchor array, something never achieved in real-world climbing. The practical aim is load distribution, knowing the load is never evenly divided. A pre-distributed anchor means the system can accept loading in one specific direction. A self-adjusting anchor can adjust to loading within a range of directional changes (multidirectional).

- **Simple** harks back to Occam's razor or the law of parsimony—the simplest solution is often best. This is especially useful when building anchors, which otherwise can get needlessly cluttered and complex. Experienced climbers know time management is crucial on multipitch routes. Remember the KISS principle: Keep It Simple, Stupid.

Key STRANDS Points

- STRANDS is an evaluation strategy, not a checklist.
- To truly assess the anchor system, the STRANDS principle must be combined with assessment criteria for the individual placements (i.e., SOS for nuts, SPORT for cams).
- Modern rigging techniques cannot compensate for insecure primary placements.
- With strong primary placements and modern rigging techniques providing security, climbing's roped safety system is typically very reliable.

Climbers on the Totem Pole, Tasman National Park, Australia
© GETTY IMAGES/CAVEN IMAGES

Step-by-Step Belay Anchor

- On popular routes the belay stances/ledges are usually well established (though not always ideal). Belay there.

- Further narrow your belay site to the most secure, ergonomic, and practical position.

- Locate suitable cracks or rock features to fashion a "good enough" belay anchor.

- Set the most bombproof, primary big nut or camming device you can find—preferably a multidirectional placement—and clip yourself in before building the rest of the anchor.

- Determine the direction(s) of pull for both the climber following the pitch and the leader casting off on the next lead.

- Simply and efficiently shore up the primary placement with secondary anchors.

- Try to set the secondary placements in close, but not cramped, proximity.

- If the rock is less than perfect, spread out the anchors, using several features, to preserve redundancy.

- Using modern rigging techniques, connect the various components of the system so they function as one unit to safeguard against all possible directions of pull.

- When bringing up a second after leading a pitch, situate your body directly in line between the anchors and the anticipated direction of pull. Remember ABC: Anchor-Belayer-Climber.

- Anchors should be timely—strive to adhere to the KISS principle: Keep It Simple, Stupid. Avoid overbuilding.

Cordelettes

A Standard Cordelette

- Is a statically equalized system that is most effective when its arms are of equal length.
- Normally consists of an 18-foot piece of 7 mm nylon cord tied into a loop with a double fisherman's knot, or 5.5 mm or 6 mm high-tensile cord connected with a triple fisherman's knot.

One method for carrying your cordelette is to start by quadrupling it (upper photo), then tie a figure-8 knot (lower photo).

Rigging a Cordelette

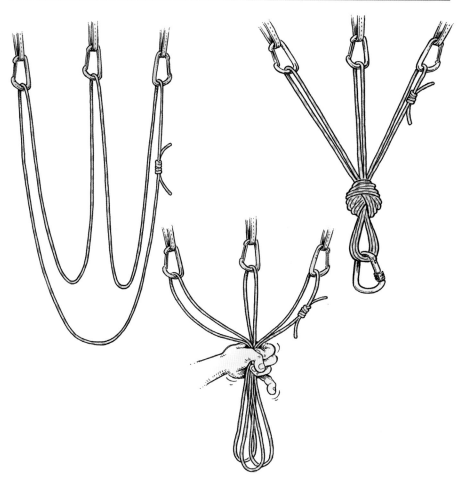

To rig a cordelette, first clip the cordelette into the primary anchors, then pull the loops of cord down between each of the pieces. Next, pull the arms of the cordelette tight toward the anticipated loading direction (direction of pull). Make sure to align the fisherman's knot so it is just below the highest placement in the system, free and clear of the master point knot. Secure the master point with an overhand knot or, if you have enough cord, a figure eight knot (as shown here). Tie the master point loop about 4 inches in diameter, roughly the same size as the belay loop on your harness. Attach a locking carabiner and clip to the master point with a section of the climbing rope, not a daisy chain, PAS, or other sling made of static material.

V Rigging

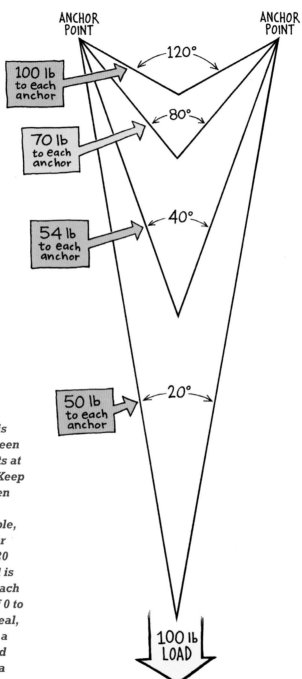

ANCHOR POINT

ANCHOR POINT

120°

100 lb to each anchor

80°

70 lb to each anchor

40°

54 lb to each anchor

20°

50 lb to each anchor

100 lb LOAD

This diagram illustrates how a 100-pound load is distributed between two anchor points at various angles. Keep the angle between two anchors as narrow as possible, striving for under 60 degrees. At 120 degrees the load is 100 percent on each anchor! Think of 0 to 60 degrees as ideal, 60 to 90 degrees a caution zone, and over 90 degrees a danger zone.

V Rigging vs. Triangle Rigging

Load per anchor with 100 lb. of force

Bottom Angle	V Rigging	Triangle Rigging
30 degrees	52 lb.	82 lb.
60 degrees	58 lb.	100 lb.
90 degrees	71 lb.	131 lb.
120 degrees	100 lb.	193 lb.
150 degrees	193 lb.	380 lb.

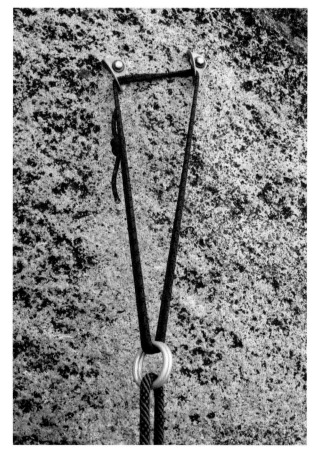

This triangle rigging configuration is known as the American triangle. Although the red cord is doubled, and there are two rap rings, the anchor is nonredundant because the red cord is just a single rethreaded cord. Avoid rigging with a triangle configuration; it adds unnecessary forces to your anchor points. Stick to a V configuration for lower loads (see chart above).

V rigging on a two-bolt toprope anchor, using a 48-inch nylon sling tied off with a figure eight knot, with locking carabiners on the bolt hangers and two pear-shaped locking carabiners at the master point. Simple, strong, and redundant.

Belay anchor with three SLCDs tied off with a cordelette. The granite is sound, and all three cams are bomber, well retracted (over 50 percent) and with all the cams nicely contacting the walls of the crack. The rope is attached to the master point with two carabiners opposed and reversed (including one locking). Clean, simple, and strong. The bottom cam means this anchor could also withstand an upward force.

Note that load equalization over placements set in a vertical crack is much more a concept than a fact. Here the bulk of direct, downward loading will fall on the middle SLCD.

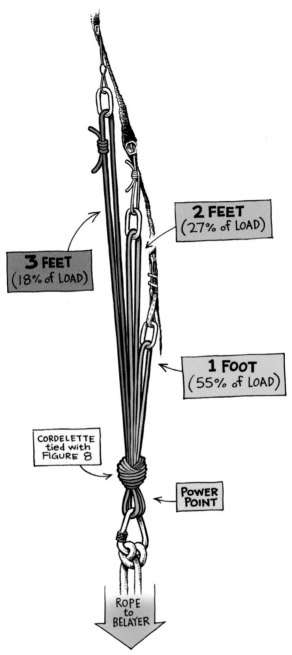

3 FEET
(18% of LOAD)

2 FEET
(27% of LOAD)

1 FOOT
(55% of LOAD)

CORDELETTE
tied with
FIGURE 8

POWER
POINT

ROPE
to
BELAYER

Using a nylon cordelette to connect anchors in a vertical crack results in an anchor that does not come close to truly equalizing the forces, but if all the placements are bomber, it is a simple, easy rigging method that is essentially a series of backups to the piece that takes the brunt of the loading, with minimal extension if that piece were to fail.

A three-piece belay anchor in a vertical crack at the top of a climb on Suicide Rock in California. Simple, quick, and easy rigging with a 7 mm nylon cordelette. This anchor is at the top of the climb, so the highest force would simply be holding the falling follower. In a vertical configuration such as this, with a nylon cordelette, the shortest loop of the cordelette (to the lowest piece) would absorb most of the load. Note how the double fisherman's knot has been placed on the longest loop near the top piece, to keep it out of the way for tying the overhand loop to create the master point.

This four-cam anchor, rigged with a cordelette, is virtually multidirectional, meaning it can withstand a pull in multiple directions: upward, downward, and to either side.

This cordelette has been unknotted and used in the "full length" mode. This is a trick adopted by many professional guides to add greater utility and get more usable length from their cordelette, particularly useful if the placements are spread out more than arm's length. Most guides prefer the flat overhand knot (with a long tail—minimum 5 inches) to initially tie their cordelette into a loop. The flat overhand is a relatively weak knot, and its failure mode is when the tails are too short and the knot capsizes (rolls inward on itself). To prevent this possibility, simply tie a second overhand

(continued)

(continued from previous page)

knot right on top of the first one as a fail-safe backup. Another good knot to use is the Flemish bend (aka figure-8 bend), tied by taking one end of the cordelette and tying a figure-8 (with a 3-inch tail) then retracing it with the other end (leaving a 3-inch tail). The figure-8 bend is stronger than a flat overhand but slightly more difficult to untie once weighted.

When untied, the cord works well for connecting three points when a standard cordelette, describing a single loop, would be too short. To rig three points, tie a figure-8 loop on each end, clip these into the two outside pieces, then clip a strand into the middle point. Pull down the cord between the pieces and you'll end up with a loop to the middle point, and a single strand to each outside piece. Then gather the two bights together and tie a two-loop master point with a figure-8.

In this particular setup the top left piece has been extended with a sling so the three arms of the cordelette are more equal length. The middle cordelette loop is clipped to two placements used together, and the right placement's carabiner has been doubled (opposed and reversed) to prevent the gate from opening over the edge of the crack. As is always the case with such setups, this one is rigged for a downward pull, and any oblique loading will put all the load on only one of the cordelette's arms.

Facing page: Three camming devices in a horizontal crack connected with a cordelette. Note how the farthest left loop has been clove-hitched to the piece to keep the fisherman's knot out of the way. As with all pre-distributed anchors, the setup is set for a single direction of pull. Even the slightest oblique angle of pull will load one side of the triangle while the other side will bear little if any load. Stretchy nylon cord is more forgiving in this regard, but off-axis loading will still weight one of the placements over the others. However, because the arms of the cordelette are of relatively equal length here, climbers can expect to achieve some equalization as long as the direction of pull is straight down.

Three-piece cordelette anchor. Note how the cams are positioned so the stems are not bent over the lip of the crack.

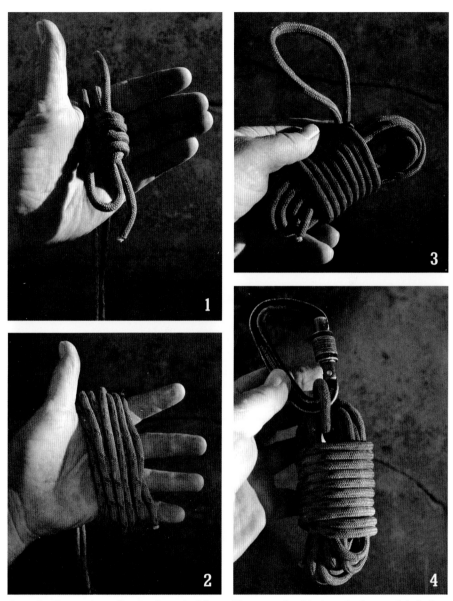

Less bulky and easily deployed, this coiling method is handy for multipitch climbing.

The Sliding X

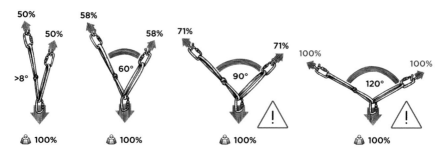

Consequences of angles in self-adjusting anchor systems

When rigging a sliding X, make sure you clip into the loop you've created by twisting the sling.

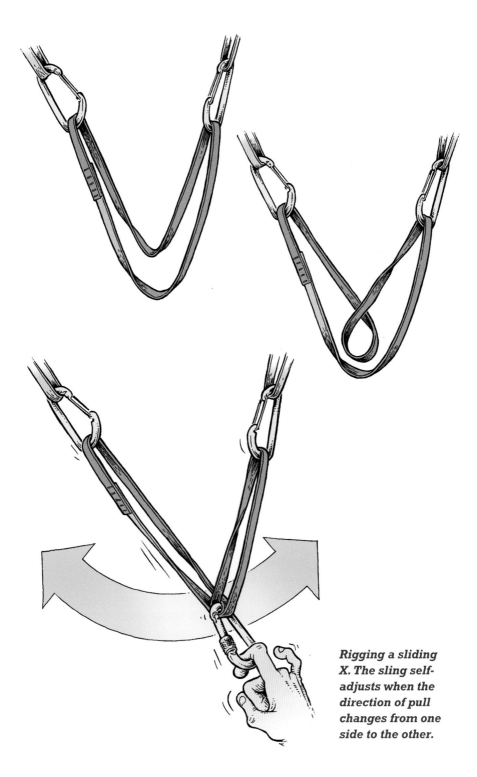

Rigging a sliding X. The sling self-adjusts when the direction of pull changes from one side to the other.

Because there is no knot on the locking carabiner side of the sling, this setup is not redundant, since you're relying on a single, twisted loop in the webbing.

Two-bolt toprope anchor rigged with a sliding X and extension-limiting knots. By using a double-length (48-inch) nylon sling tied with two overhand knots, the sling itself becomes redundant at the master point, since it has two loops of webbing.

Two cam placements rigged with a sliding X with extension-limiting knots, set up as a component part of a larger toprope anchor system. By using a double-length (48-inch) nylon sling and tying two overhand knots, the sling itself becomes redundant.

Stacked X's. Here, by tying the two overhand knots on the purple sling, extension is limited and redundancy is achieved.

Detail of two-bolt sliding X anchor rigging with two separate Dyneema slings for redundancy, with three ovals opposed and reversed (left photo), and two pear-shaped locking carabiners opposed and reversed (right photo).

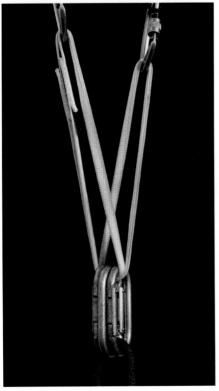

Three camming devices rigged with a sliding X and clove hitches. This is a good belay anchor rig for a multipitch climb, providing the two climbers are swinging leads. Since there is no masterpoint, climbers swapping leads at this belay stance will require the arriving climber to also rig his rope in this fashion. No big deal, but a bit more time consuming, and a real cluster if there were a third climber at this stance. If one of the two SLCDs on top were to blow out, there would be sudden loading on the remaining anchor. Judging by the placements (A1), however, this would be nearly impossible, even in a factor-2 fall situation, as the downward force would be shared by the two cams, and the force required to break the sling would be astronomical.

A tricky belay anchor on Mechanic's Route, Tahquitz Rock, California. The top two pieces are rigged with a sliding X, with an overhand knot tied to limit any extension to the top piece. The double-length red nylon sling is tied with a figure-8 to create redundancy at the master point.

A two-cam anchor on Tahquitz Rock, rigged with a sliding X using two separate slings. While making three separate placements is a dogmatic goal for gear anchors, consider one of the most common anchors on face climbs: two bolts. Here we have perfect rock structure—immaculate, fine-grained granite—and two perfect Camalot placements. Should we trust this anchor? Absolutely. Each Camalot has a breaking strength of 12 kN (2,698 lb.), each sling is rated at 22 kN (nearly 5,000 lb.), and two opposed and reversed carabiners are stronger than that. Know your equipment, its breaking strengths, and how it all adds up. A good rule of thumb is for your anchor to be no weaker than 24 kN (5,395 lb.).

The Quad

Tying the Quad

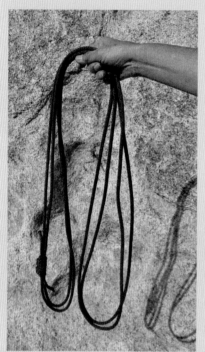 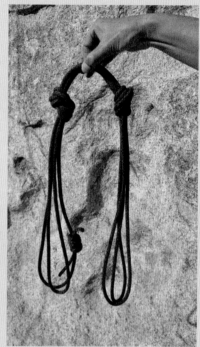

To tie the quad, an 18- to 20-foot cordelette or 240 cm sling works best. Start by doubling the sling or cordelette then grab the middle with one hand. If using a cordelette, position the knot (or if using a sling, the sewn connection for the sling) toward the end of the doubled loop. Tie an overhand knot on each side of your hand and you're done.

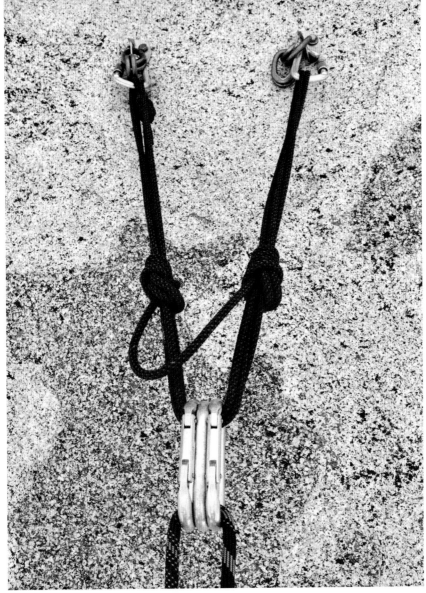

Two-bolt quad rigged for a toprope setup. Lab testing suggests that for two horizontally oriented anchor points (as shown here), the quad setup is basically indestructible. Field testing suggests that for those who frequently belay from, or toprope off, two horizontally oriented bolts (as found on top of countless sport and toprope climbs), a quad rig is your best friend. Simply keep a quad rigged (with the limiter knots tied) on a piece of 7 mm nylon or 5 or 6 mm high-strength cord and break it out for use in these situations. Brute strength and fantastic load distribution are achieved just as quickly as you can clip off the bolts and the master point.

Here locking carabiners are attached directly to the bolt hangers, bypassing the hardware store rappelling doodads, and three oval carabiners (opposed and reversed) are used for the rope attachment.

Quad rigged for toproping with two locking carabiners opposed and reversed

Quad rig close-up. At 12.4 kN (2,788 lb.) tensile strength for each strand of this Sterling 7 mm cordelette, clipping just two strands at the master point gives you twice the strength ever needed. Clip three and have a submarine anchor. Just make sure you leave one strand unclipped (as shown here) to create a loop for your master point, so that if one of the anchors were to fail, the loop would capture the carabiners.

A quad rig using Sterling 6 mm PowerCord and three steel oval carabiners for a toprope setup

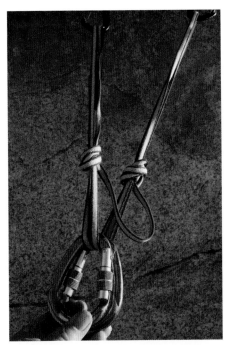

Two-bolt quad anchor rigged with a 240 cm sling and two pear-shaped locking carabiners for toproping. Start by doubling the sling, grab the midpoint with your fist, then tie loose overhand knots on both sides of your fist. Adjust the knots as needed. When using a pair of locking carabiners at the master point, pear-shaped carabiners work best due to their symmetry, centering the rope at the midpoint of the carabiners' basket, reducing shifting and rubbing of the gate-locking mechanisms.

Example of another method for rigging a quad using two separate single-length slings, matched together, then tied with overhand knots, rigged here with two pear-shaped locking carabiners for a toproping setup

Two-bolt anchor rigged with a quad using two separate single-length Dyneema slings, with three oval carabiners opposed and reversed, clipped into three of the four master point strands for toproping

By splitting the four strands, two and two, the quad offers two separate, redundant master points, great for belaying from single- or multipitch anchors. To use the quad on a multipitch anchor, split the end loops two and two, giving you two separate but redundant master points.

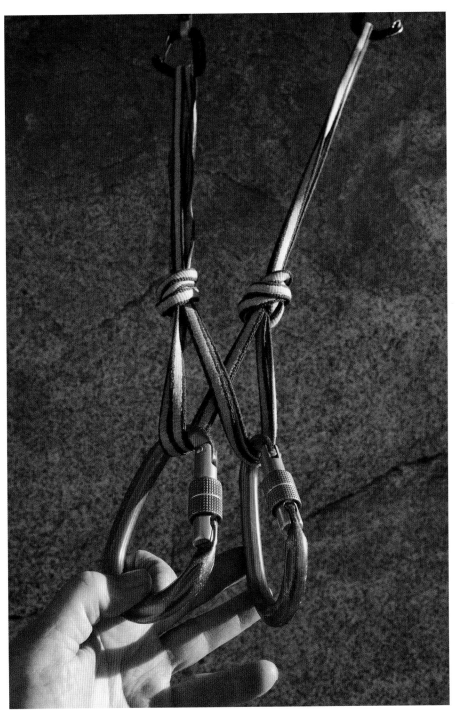

240-cm Dyneema sling rigged as a two-point quad belay anchor

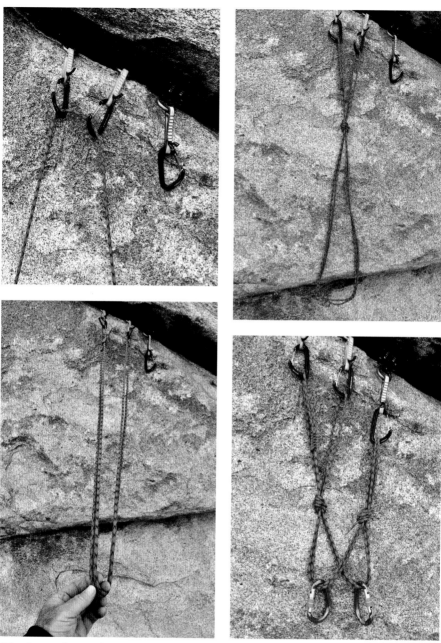

Rigging a three-piece belay anchor with the quad. Clip a single loop into two pieces. Pull the cordelette down between the two pieces in the anticipated direction of pull. Even out the loops, then tie an overhand knot. Tie a similar overhand knot and clip to the third piece. Ideally, the third piece should be strongest. Now you have two redundant master points.

Three-point anchor rigged with a quad for a direct belay

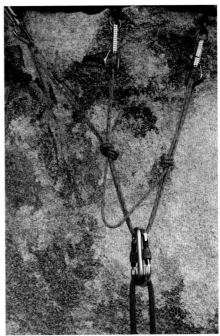

Three-point toproping anchor rigged with a quad. The two locking carabiners are opposed and reversed and clipped into three of the four master point strands.

Belay station with three-point quad rigging. Here the belayer is belaying his second. He's anchored to the left two strands with a clove hitch on a locking carabiner and belaying from the right two strands with an autoblocking device (Petzl Reverso).

Composite Anchors: Cordelette, Sliding X, and Quad

Multipitch anchor with cordelette and sliding X combo. While this setup—and ones like it—have been a mainstay for many years, incorporating new techniques such as the quad will allow climbers to achieve even better load distribution.

A three-piece anchor using a combination of quad and sliding X rigging

Upward Oppositional Anchors

This rig shows a cordelette used to distribute the load on two nuts combined with two SLCDs clove-hitched to provide opposition. A belayer tied tight to these anchors isn't going to be lifted any more than 18 inches—enough to provide some give in the system but not enough to be dangerous.

Simple three-piece multipitch anchor rigged with an upward directional piece

Multipitch belay at Tahquitz Rock, California. The leader is ready to go, and the belayer has put him on belay. When the leader unclips his clove hitch, he'll clip his rope to the top piece, which already has a quickdraw waiting. The leader's rope is butterfly-looped and ready to pay out without any tangles. Once up on the pitch, if the leader falls, the upward force on the belayer would soften the impact, and the right-hand piece in the anchor, placed for an upward pull, would keep the belayer from getting yanked too far upward.

Keys to building belay anchors:

- Find a belay that provides convenient anchor placements and suitable positions for the climbing team, once the anchor is set.

- An ideal belay system limits peak loading through the dynamic qualities in the system. The give and flex of the belayer's body, the stretch in the cordelette or slings and, first and foremost, the elasticity in the lead rope, all serve to gently slow down the accelerating mass, as opposed to stopping it all at once, like a head-on collision.

- After selecting a location and securing yourself to that first placement, take a moment to plan the entire system. Analyze the situation and fashion the anchors to withstand loading from all possible directions of pull.

- Keep the system as simple as possible, so it is quick to set and easy to double-check and monitor. Use the minimal amount of gear to safely and efficiently do the job, which is usually three or four bombproof anchors, more if they are less than ideal.

- The placements are only as strong as the rock they are set in.

- Strive to make anchors meet the STRANDS criteria: Solid (Rock and Placements), Timely, Redundant, Angles (less than 90 degrees), No Extension, Distributes Load, and Simple.

Facing page: Here the belay device is clipped into the belay loop on the climber's harness—an indirect belay. Providing the belayer has a solid stance to brace against downward loading, the indirect belay is the technique of choice if the anchor is less than superb. In holding a fall the belayer, not the anchor, bears the brunt of the fall force, which can be uncomfortable and awkward when the falling climber hangs on the rope for a long period of time. Although this belay method is probably the most common method used by recreational climbers to belay a follower, it is rarely used by professional guides, who favor the direct belay as long as the anchor is bomber.

Though not always possible, the ideal is: With any indirect belay the belayer should try to get into a position directly beneath the belay anchor to avoid getting dragged there by downward loading. Remember ABC positioning for bringing up the second: Anchor-Belayer-Climber.

Here the belay device is clipped into both the harness's belay loop and the loop in the figure-8 tie-in knot. If the climber falls, most of his weight will go onto the anchor, not on the belayer—providing that the belayer is situated directly beneath the anchor. To the extent that the belayer is to one side or the other of the anchor is the extent that his body, not the anchor, will bear the load.

This shows how a redirected belay is set up. Always remember that a redirect basically doubles the loading on the anchor—no problem with premium anchors (like bolts on a sport climb), but with sketchy anchors a re-directed belay is a little dicey. Here a bomber four-piece anchor is rigged with a cordelette, and the redirect is run through the master point.

This effectively illustrates a clean and simple rigging of a direct belay (direct belay = belaying directly off the belay anchor) via a Petzl Grigri clipped into the master point. Note how the master point is at an ergonomically friendly chest level, ideal for managing a direct belay. Tube devices, such as the Petzl Reverso and the Black Diamond ATC Guide, can also be used for direct belaying in the autoblocking mode. You DO NOT, however, want to use an ordinary tube device (like a regular ATC) for a direct belay, as the brake position would be awkward and potentially dangerous, especially if the master point is waist level or higher. Another direct belay option is to use a Munter hitch on a large, pear-shaped locking carabiner.

    Remember: A direct belay is an easy and efficient means to belay the second or follower, but it should not be used to belay the leader on a trad climb. Also understand that with all direct belays, when the anchors are less than ideal, any loading bypasses the shock-absorbing qualities of the belayer's body and places the entire load directly onto the anchors. Granted, toprope forces are generally moderate, but any force is a concern if you've wandered off route and get stuck belaying from marginal gear. When the anchors are rock solid, however, a direct belay is a quick, efficient, and comfortable way to bring up a second.

Lowering with a Grigri and a direct belay. Here the belayer is clove-hitched to the shelf of the cordelette (all three loops of the cordelette's arms). To lower someone using a Grigri, redirect the brake strand as shown here for better control on the lower. This is an awkward maneuver unless the master point is rigged waist level or higher. Remember, even with an assisted braking device like a Grigri, never take your brake hand off the brake-strand side of the rope when belaying or lowering someone.

Three-bolt anchor rigged for a direct belay using a Grigri. Here the Grigri is clipped to a locking carabiner clipped to the shelf (all three loops of the cordelette's arms). The leader has clipped directly into the bolt hangers, bypassing the old hardware store quick links.

Guides frequently use a rope-direct belay when the anchor is set back from the edge and they want to position themselves near the edge to eyeball their client. In this setup you run the rope through two carabiners at the anchor's master point, climb down to the edge, then tie an overhand loop on the doubled bight of rope. This now serves as an extended master point, and the belayer is secured where he wants to be. Here a Grigri is used for a direct belay from the new master point.

Another clean and simple rigging for a rope-direct belay. Take the rope from your harness and tie a clove hitch to the master point carabiner, then, off the back side of the clove hitch, tie a figure-8 loop and clip back to the anchor with a separate carabiner. The direct belay goes off this strand (on another figure-8 loop), and it can be any distance from the anchor (e.g., 20 or 30 feet away), to allow you to position yourself so you can see the follower. You'll always be able to give a better belay if you can get a visual on your climber.

When belaying your second on a single pitch climb, if your anchor is set well back from the edge, by extending your rope connection to the anchor you can position yourself at the edge, establishing visual contact with your partner. This allows you to give the best belay: controlling slack and taking in rope as they move up. Climbers on Looning the Tube (5.9), Gwynedd, North Wales.

For belaying a second from the top of a single-pitch route, the Atomic Clip is a simple and efficient rigging method. It is particularly useful for belaying from two-bolt anchors. Tie a double-loop bowline or double-loop eight, clip it to the two anchor points, and equalize it. Here the climber is using a direct belay with a Grigri clipped to a figure-8 loop on the strand running from the back side of the double-loop bowline.

CHAPTER NINE

Toprope Anchors

Tips for Setting

- Evaluate any hazards at the site, especially loose rocks that the movement of a running rope could dislodge.

- Extend the anchors over the edge at the top of the cliff to prevent rope drag and damage. Professional guides prefer to rig this extension with a length of low-stretch or static rope. Pad any sharp edges at the lip. Make sure the rope sits directly above the climb, and make sure to run two independent strands of rope or webbing over the lip to maintain redundancy.

- Set the chocks and SLCDs fairly close together near the top of the climb when possible to reduce the number of slings and carabiners required.

- Avoid setting pieces behind detached blocks, flakes, or other questionable rock features. Avoid having the rope near these features.

- Connect the rope to the master point with two opposed and reversed locking carabiners or three ovals.

- Belay toprope climbs from the ground whenever possible.

- Avoid belaying directly below the climber, in case rocks come off.

- A ground anchor merely needs to provide extra ballast to help you counterweight the climber, so one bombproof piece is usually sufficient.

- If you're in an exposed situation where getting yanked from your ground belay would be disastrous or even fatal, set up a redundant anchor system.

Bomber toprope anchor. Clean, simple, and strong. The bolts are ⅜-inch diameter five-piece Power Bolts (7,000 lb. shear strength) installed with Fixe ring anchors (rated at 10,000 lb.). The 7 mm nylon Sterling cordelette (rated at 5,000 lb. loop strength tied with a double fisherman's bend) is doubled then tied with an overhand knot, leaving a four-loop master point. The rope is attached with three steel oval carabiners opposed and reversed. If you do a lot of toproping like Bob does, steel is far more durable than aluminum. As discussed earlier, any off-axis loading will put most or all of the force on one bolt, but in toprope situations the forces are relatively low (compared to a leader fall) and the extension would be minimal even if one of the bolts failed. Plus a nylon cordelette (versus a Dyneema or Technora cord) has some modicum of stretch, resulting in a lower force than if using more static material.

A quad rigged for toproping with two locking carabiners opposed and reversed

A two-bolt anchor rigged for toproping with a sliding X. Note the locking carabiners on the bolt hangers, two separate nylon slings, and three steel ovals. Bob rigged this anchor for adjustment since he'd be toproping three different routes off the same anchor, each in a slightly different direction. A good rule of thumb regarding extension is this: Limit extension in any anchor system to no more than half a single-length sling.

The Joshua Tree System

Developed by professional guides at Joshua Tree National Park, the Joshua Tree System greatly simplifies seemingly complex toprope anchor setups. Bob has used it for over 30 years in his climbing school and can vouch for its efficiency and security. Using this system, he's never come across a climb he couldn't rig a toprope on, as long as there was enough rope. For most situations a length of 50 to 60 feet is adequate. Bob's favorite brands are the 10 mm diameter Sterling *Safety Pro* and the 10 mm diameter Beal *Spelenium.* These brands have about 4 percent stretch under a 300 lb. load, with good abrasion resistance. You don't want to use dynamic rope for your rigging rope, because it is easily abraded due to its stretch, and far less abrasion resistant than static or low-stretch rope.

To rig the Joshua Tree System, visualize a V configuration, with the two separate anchors at the top of the V and your master point at the point, or bottom, of the V. For your master point knot, learn the BHK (page 130). BHK stands for "big honking knot" and is essentially an overhand knot on a doubled bight, giving you two-loop redundancy at the master point.

The combinations of various anchors are endless, and if you learn double-loop knots (like the double-loop eight and double-loop bowline), you'll be able to rig without slings and cordelettes, using only the rigging rope.

Tether detail. If you're working at the cliff's edge, protect yourself. This climber has rigged his BHK master point, all the while protected with a personal tether—a double-length nylon sling. He's secured one end to his harness with a locking carabiner; the other end is attached to the rigging rope via a klemheist knot.

Overview of the Joshua Tree System. The left leg of the extension rope is attached with a double-loop bowline to two cams; the right leg is clovehitched to a single, bomber cam. A BHK is tied for the master point, with three opposed and reversed oval carabiners ready for the climbing rope.

Rigging the Joshua Tree System. After the anchor placements were made, the climber pre-distributed the bottom leg of the V with a double-loop eight. As he approached the edge, he secured himself by tethering with a sling to a prusik knot on the rigging rope. He's tying the BHK master point knot, to which he'll attach the carabiners for the climbing rope. He'll make the final adjustment with a clove hitch to the top anchor and fix an edge protector to safeguard against wear at the lip.

The Joshua Tree System rigged using double-loop figure-8s. Note how the climber is tethered with a double-length nylon sling attached to the rigging rope with a klemheist knot.

Another version of the Joshua Tree System. Here, both legs have two cams rigged with sliding X's—an elaborate rig but one that fully adjusts to any shift, however minor, in the direction of pull. In most setups, double-loop knots are preferable; they're more efficient, and since you know the direction the anchor will be loaded, drastic vector changes are not a concern.

Illustration of how to rig the Joshua Tree System using double-loop knots (in this case, double-loop figure-8s), with two anchor placements at each leg of the V.

Above: Detail of BHK master point with three ovals opposed and reversed on a toprope setup.

Left: A rope protector like this Petzl model (made of ballistic cloth with Velcro closure) can save your rigging rope from getting frayed over edges. Attach it with a friction hitch—like the klemheist knot shown here.

Facing page bottom: Rig an autoblock out of 3 feet, 9 inches of the softest, most supple 6 mm nylon cord you can find, tied with a double fisherman's knot. An autoblock is simply a wrap, with both ends of the loop clipped to a carabiner.

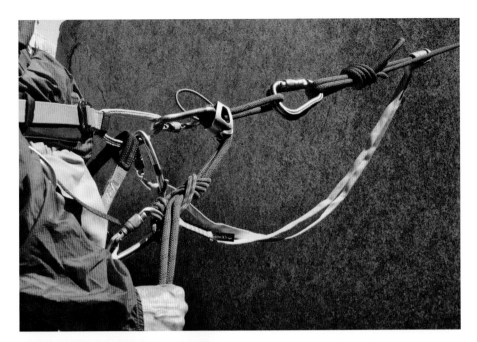

Making the transition from rigging to rappelling. Once you're done rigging and choose to rappel down, secure yourself with a tether by using a 48-inch nylon sling attached to the rigging rope with a klemheist knot and clipped to the belay loop of your harness with a locking carabiner. Before you go over the edge, pull up the climbing rope, rig your rappel, and back it up with an autoblock knot clipped to your leg loop. Don't allow too much distance between the toprope master point carabiners and your rappel device, because as you go over the edge, you'll want enough slack in your double-length sling (here the yellow sling) so that you can weight your rappel system and check that your autoblock is grabbing without any weight on the sling. After double-checking everything, you should be able to reach up and untie the klemheist so you can take the sling with you.

Tying a BHK

Take a bight of rope and double it.

Tie an overhand knot on all four strands.

Thread the two loops back through the single loop you've created.

Or incorporate the loop into the master point carabiners.

Joshua Tree System rigged off three gear placements

Two-bolt anchor rigged with the Joshua Tree System with three oval carabiners.

CHAPTER ELEVEN

Rappel Anchors

Tips for Safety

- Statistically, rappelling is one of the most dangerous procedures in all of climbing.

- Rappelling forces you to rely completely on your equipment and anchors/rigging.

- Rappelling off the end of the rope, not displaced nuts, cams, etc., is the most common rappelling accident. Always tie a stopper knot in the end of the rope.

- Never trust, and always thoroughly check, the integrity of fixed rappel anchors (including the rigging, especially old slings), and back them up as required.

- Excepting huge trees and titanic natural features, at least two bomb-proof anchors should be established at rappel stations.

- Avoid the American triangle rigging system. Anchors should be rigged using weight-distributed slings or at least slings of equal length.

- Never run the rope around a chain connecting the anchors.

- Double-check all connecting links (anchor placements/slings, slings/rope, rope/rappel device, rappel device/harness) before you weight the system and start down.

- Always rappel slowly and smoothly to keep a low, static load on the anchor. Bouncing and sudden stops cause the peak loading to spike alarmingly.

Above: A bomber two-bolt rappel anchor consisting of ½-inch stainless-steel Powers five-piece bolts (10,000-pound shear strength each) with Fixe stainless-steel hangers (25k N) and welded, stainless-steel rings (25 kN). This is a suitable setup for a minimal use anchor (used for occasional rappelling) but a poor choice for a high-traffic anchor because once the rings wear out (and they do after enough ropes are pulled through them), they are more difficult to replace.

Top right: A well-engineered three-bolt anchor on a popular sport climb at Joshua Tree. All the components are stainless steel and the quick links (which unlike welded rings, can be wrenched open) allow easy replacement of the rings, once they show signs of wear.

Bottom right: A modern rappel anchor. All components are stainless steel, including ½-inch Power-Bolts and Fixe hangers with welded chain and rings.

Not your hardware store variety, these CE-certified quick links were made for climbing applications. Top: Camp stainless-steel 8 mm (rated at 50 kN MBS or 11,240 lb.); bottom: Petzl stainless-steel Maillon Rapide (SWL 1,400 kg or 3,086 lb.—SWL stands for safe working load, typically one-fifth of the breaking strength).

SMC rap rings are light (11 g) and strong (14 kN/3,147 lb.), a good choice for carrying on long multipitch climbs where weight is a factor and the descent will involve multiple rappels. Always use two for redundancy. They are a poor choice for high-use fixed anchors, as aluminum wears quickly.

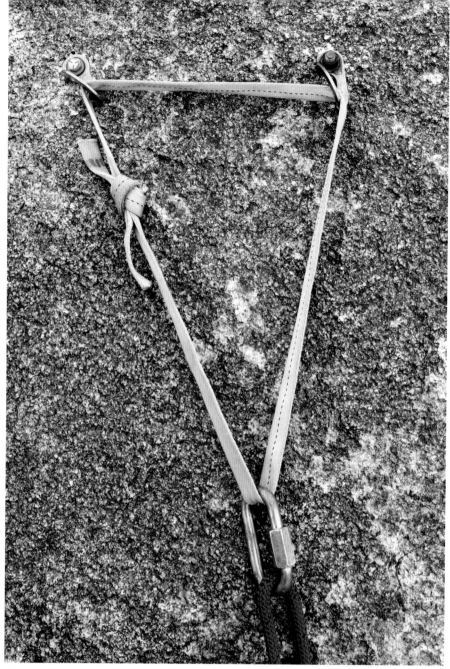

Two-bolt anchor with American triangle rigging, with a single, nonredundant sling and single, hardware store quick link. Triangle rigging is poor engineering. With triangle rigging, if the bottom angle is 60 degrees, with a 200-pound load each bolt will be loaded to around 200 pounds. With V rigging, however, the same 200-pound load would place only 116 pounds of load on each bolt. Always require redundancy in your rappel anchor, which we don't have in this poor setup.

Better (and redundant) rigging with two slings rigged individually. This example shows V rigging on one of the most common rappel anchors you'll encounter—a two-bolt anchor. Here we have two separate 1-inch nylon slings, tied with water knots and two rap rings. With this narrow of an angle, the load is distributed nearly 50/50 on the bolts. Simple, strong, and redundant.

This two-bolt rap anchor is well engineered. All the components are stainless steel. Both bolts are five-piece Powers. The left one has a stainless-steel Fixe hanger with stainless chain attached to a final quick link; the right bolt has a Petzl hanger with a quick link/welded stainless ring combo. The positioning of the bolts combined with the hardware rigging makes for a narrow angle of pull between the two bolts. Good to go.

Two-bolt rap anchor in a mountain environment, exposed to winter snow and ice. The bolts are ⅜-inch buttonhead drives. The hangers, being made of stainless steel, appear fine, but the carbon steel quick links show corrosion that has started to take hold like a slow-growing cancer, only 9 years after installation. The welded stainless rings also show signs of wear—right at the welds.

Although the paint job has worn off, this rap anchor combo shows no signs of corrosion, even after many years in a mountain environment. That's because all the components—bolts, hangers, quick links, and rings—are made of quality stainless steel. It's more expensive to install a setup like this, but it will likely be good for a hundred years.

Slings through a thread at Joshua Tree National Park. The rigging is redundant, but how strong is the rock itself? It's really just a pinch where two massive blocks touch, forming a keyhole that the slings are threaded through. Use discretion with blocks. Remember, you want a chunk of rock attached to the planet, not one sitting on top of the planet.

Typical rigging found at many climbing areas that have trees: two separate 1-inch nylon webbing slings, each tied with a water knot, and two rappel rings. Be skeptical of fixed slings. Check to make sure the knots are tied correctly, the webbing is supple, the color is not faded, and there are no burns or tears.

This sturdy rock bollard is attached to the main structure of the cliff, and the rigging is redundant, with two new separate 1-inch tubular nylon slings and two rappel rings. Bomber.

This sling was damaged by a rappel rope being retrieved. The friction of the rope being pulled across the sling generated heat, partially melting and damaging the sling's fibers. A sling in this condition has lost most of its strength.

"Tat" is climber's slang for old slings left at an anchor. On this desert rappel anchor the slings, although numerous, are all stiff and degraded, and the color has faded from years in the sun. The master point is a single, hardware store quick link, making the entire anchor nonredundant. If you find yourself on trad routes that necessitate rappels from natural features such as trees and rock features, prepare yourself with a small knife, some spare nylon webbing, and rap rings to rerig old tat like this.

The removed webbing from the above anchor reveals remarkable UV light degradation plus burn marks where a rope has been pulled over the webbing. In tests of old nylon slings that are degraded by years of UV exposure, some had lost almost all their strength.

Rappel from the Shark's Fin. Alabama Hills, California.
© GETTY IMAGES/DAVID KEATON

For the Last Time . . .

The best rigging can do no more than exploit the potential holding strength of the primary placements. Hence the first rule in building all anchors is to get sound primary placements. With bomber primary placements, the rules of thumb and modern rigging methods stack the odds in your favor that the anchor will do its job and do it well.

Index

Italicized page numbers indicate illustrations.

A

ABC (Anchor-Belayer-Climber) positioning, 108
American triangle rigging, 79, *79*, *133, 136*
anchor building basics, 1, 142
anchor systems
    assessment criteria for, 74
    evaluation principles for, 73–74
    rappel anchors, 133, *134, 135, 136, 137, 138, 139, 140*
    toproping, *92, 97, 103,* 117–20, *118, 119, 120*
    See also belay anchors; Joshua Tree System
angles
    as anchor system evaluation principle, 73
    preferred, for cords/slings, *2*
    of sliding X, *90*
    for V rigging systems, *78*
Atomic Clip, *116*
"attached to the planet," 8, *139*
autoblocking devices, *103, 111,* 128, 129, *129*
autoblocking knots, 129

B

bartacked sewn webbing loops, 6
Beal *Spelenium* (rope), 121
belay anchors
    belaying methods with, 108, *109, 110, 111, 112, 113, 114, 115, 116*
    building tips, 108
    composites, *104*

cordelette rigging systems for, 77, *81, 82, 83, 84, 85–87, 88*
directions of pull and, 57
fall forces and, 51, *53, 54*
multipitch, *104, 106, 107*
placement step-by-step strategies, 75
quad, *96, 97, 98, 99. 100, 101, 102, 103*
sliding X, 90, *90, 91, 92, 93, 94, 95*
upward oppositional, 105, *105, 106*
V rigging, *78, 79, 80*
See also belaying
belaying
    with Atomic Clips, *116*
    direct, *111, 112*
    fall factor calculations, *52*
    fall forces and load limiting, 51
    indirect, 108, *109*
    redirected, *110*
    rope-direct, *113, 114*
    tips for, *115*
    with toprope anchors, 117
BHKs (big honking knots)
    Joshua Tree System using, 121, *121, 123, 124, 128*
    tying instructions, *130*
Black Diamond ATC Guide, *111*
Black Diamond Camalots
    cam placement recommendations, 41
    placement assessments using, *31, 34, 35, 36, 40, 41*
    sliding X belay anchors with, *95*
Black Diamond Hexes, *26*
Black Diamond Micro Stoppers, *22, 23*
Black Diamond Stoppers, *14, 15, 16, 17*

bolts
   materials recommended for, *43*
   placement strategies, *44, 48*
   quads with two-bolt rigging, 97
   for rappel anchors, 134
   safety assessments, *44, 47, 48,*
      49, 50
   styles and types of, *43, 44, 45*
bottleneck nut placements, *15, 16, 18*
boulders and blocks, 7, *7, 8, 13,*
      42, 117
bowline knots
   double-loop (bowline-on-a-bight),
      66, 116, 121, *123*
   for natural anchor rigging, *6, 12*
   requirements of, *6*
   tying instructions, *65*
bowline-on-a-bight (double-loop bow-
      line knots), *66, 116,* 121, *123*
butterfly-looped ropes, *107*
buttonhead contraction bolts, *45, 48,*
      49, 138

C

camming devices (cams, spring loaded
      camming devices, SLCDs), *19,*
      42, 81. See also cam placements
cam placements
   assessment criteria acronyms for,
      30, 74
   assessments of, 30
   basic essentials for, 29, 41, 42
   belay anchor systems with, *86–87,*
      88
   color coding for, 29, 33
   good examples of, *32, 33, 34,*
      39, 40
   horizontal, 29
   poor examples of, *30, 31, 32, 34,*
      35, 36, 39, 41
   retraction ideal ranges for, *32*
cams, *19, 81. See also* cam placements

carabiners
   cam placement issues with, *37*
   cordelette rigging systems with, 77
   hitches/knots for, *70*
   Joshua Tree System using, *123*
   loading recommendations for
      doubled, *72*
   for micronut packing, *22*
   with sliding X anchor systems, *93*
   for toproping anchors, 117, *118, 119*
   types of, *72*
   See also locking carabiners; ovals
chocks. *See* nuts
chockstones, *12*
clove hitches
   for belay anchor rigging, *86–87*
   Joshua Tree System using, *123, 124*
   for oppositional nuts, *20*
   for sliding X belay anchor systems, *94*
   tying instructions, *64*
coffin nails, 50
composite belay anchors, *104*
compromises, 1
contraction bolts, *44, 48, 49, 138*
cordelettes
   belay anchor systems with, 77, *81,*
      82, 83, 84, 85–87, 88
   carrying strategies, 76
   composite anchors with, *104*
   definition and descriptions, 76
   with figure-8 loops for natural
      anchors, *2*
   for natural anchors, *9, 11*
   periodic inspections of, 42
   rigging, 77
   for toproping anchors, *118*
cords
   for horizontal placements, 29
   periodic inspections of, 42
   strength categories for, 6
   threaded through tunnel or pocket,
      11, 12, 129

corrosion
  of bolts, *49,* 50
  galvanic, *43*
  of hangers, *46, 47*
  of rappel anchor quick links, *138*
cracks
  belay anchor rigging in, *81, 82,*
    86–87
  rock assessments and, *7, 9, 11, 31*
  See also nut placements
cratering, 50

D
death hangers, *46*
deaths, *47*
detached blocks, 7, *7, 8*
directions of pull, *19,* 57, *58, 59, 60.*
    See also pre-distributed
    (equalized) anchor systems
distribution of load, 73. *See also* pre-
    distributed (equalized) anchor
    systems; sliding X
double fisherman's knots, *63, 66,*
    83, 118
double-loop bowline knots (bowline-
    on-a-bight), *66, 116,* 121, *123*
double-loop figure-8 knots, *68,* 121,
    125, 127
double-loop knots, 121, *126, 127*

E
edge (rope) protectors, *124, 128*
environmental controversies, *49*
equalized anchors. *See* pre-distributed
    (equalized) anchor systems
expansion bolts, *43, 44, 49, 118*
extension-limiting strategies
  cordelette rigging for, *82*
  guidelines for, 73
  for sliding X systems, 90, *92,*
    93, 95
  for toproping, *118, 120*

F
fall forces
  anchor systems and, *53*
  and directions of pull, *19,* 57, *58,*
    59, 60
  facts on, 51
  fall factor calculations, *52*
  protection pieces and, *51, 56*
  sliding X belay anchor systems
    placements and, *94*
figure-8 follow-through knots, *5*
figure-8 loops/knots
  for belay anchor systems, *86*
  for carrying cordelettes, *76*
  for cordelette rigging, *77, 82*
  direct belaying with, *116*
  natural anchors and cordelette
    rigging with, *2*
  for rope-direct belaying, *114*
  tying instructions, *62*
fisherman's knots
  for anchor system backup, *66*
  for belay anchor systems, *83, 86–87*
  for natural anchors, *6, 12*
  for toprope anchor systems, *118*
  tying instructions, *63*
Fixe hangers, *134, 138*
Fixe ring anchors, *118*
flakes, 7, *13, 30, 31, 42,* 117
flat overhand knots, *85, 86*
Flemish bend, *86*
friction hitches, *128*

G
galvanic corrosion, *43*
girth hitches, *5, 11, 12*
ground anchors, 117
Gunk's tie off, 29

H
hangers, *43, 46, 47, 49,* 50, *138*
Hexes (nuts), *24, 26*

hitches
    clove, *20, 64*
    girth, *5, 11, 12*
    Munter, *69*
horizontal nut placements, *17*

I

improvisation, 1

J

Jesus Nuts, 51, *56*
Joshua Tree System
    development of, 121
    knots for, 121, *121, 122, 130*
    rigging examples, 121, *123, 124,
        126, 131, 132*
    rigging to rappelling transitions
        for, *129*

K

klemheist knots, *121, 122, 125,
    128, 129*
knots
    autoblocking, 129
    BHKs (big honking knots), 121,
        121, 123, 124, 128, 130
    double-loop, 121, *126, 127*
    double-loop bowline (bowline-on-
        a-bight), *66, 116,* 121, *123*
    double-loop figure-8, *68,* 121,
        125, 127
    extension-limiting, *92*
    figure-8 follow-through, *5*
    flat overhand, *85, 86*
    Flemish bend, *86*
    friction hitches, *128*
    girth hitches, *5, 11, 12*
    klemheist, *121, 122, 125, 128, 129*
    Munter hitch, *69*
    prusik, *67, 124*
    slip, *10*
    stopper, 133

water (ring bend), 6, *61, 139*
    See also bowline knots; clove hitches;
        figure-8 loops/knots; fisherman's
        knots; overhand knots

L

leader falls, *36, 37, 53, 54, 59, 105,
    107*
Leeper hangers, *47*
load distribution, 73. *See also* pre-
    distributed (equalized) anchor
    systems; sliding X
load multiplication, *2,* 73, 90
locking carabiners
    advantages of, 72
    belaying anchors using, *54, 55,
        80, 92, 93, 97, 98, 99, 103,
        111, 112*
    cordelette rigging with, 77
    for Joshua Tree System, *121, 129*
    knots for, *69*
    toproping anchors using, 117,
        119, 120
    with two bold quad rigging, *97*
loop strength, 6

M

master points
    cordelette rigging with, 77
    fall forces and systems with, *54*
    fall potential and systems with, *54*
    toproping anchors with four-loop,
        118
Metolius hangers, *49*
Metolius Power Cams
    color coding, 29, *33*
    placement examples using, *33, 34,
        35, 36*
    retraction ranges for, *34*
micronuts, 22, *22, 23*
Moretti, Mike, *55*
multipitch belay anchors, *104, 106, 107*

Munter hitches, *69, 70*

N

natural anchors
    chockstones as, *12*
    descriptions, 3
    for rappelling, *139*
    rock assessments of, 7, *7, 8*
    rock horns as, *8, 9, 10, 11*
    rock tunnels or pockets as, *11, 12,*
        139
    trees as, *2, 4, 5, 6*
no extension, as anchor system evalu-
    ation principle, 73. *See also*
    extension-limiting strategies
nut placements
    assessment criteria acronyms for,
        13, 74
    basic rules for, 13, 41, 42
    failure causes, *16*
    graded examples of, *14, 15, 16, 17,*
        18, 25
    horizontal, *17*
    micronuts, 22, *22, 23*
    oppositional, *17, 19, 20*
    rock assessments for, *26*
    stacked, *17*
    for toprope anchors, 117
nuts (chocks)
    breaking strength reviews, *23*
    periodic inspections of, 42
    types and styles of, 22, *22, 23, 24,*
        27, 28
    See also nut placements

O

Occam's razor, 73
offset nuts, *17*
oppositional nuts, *17, 19, 20, 21*
orientation, 13, 30
ovals (carabiners)
    belay anchor systems with, *93, 97*

Joshua Tree System using, *123,*
    128, 132
    loading recommendations, 72
    toproping anchors using, *120*
overhand knots
    for cordelette rigging, 77
    for cordelettes on natural anchors, *9*
    disadvantages and backups for,
        85–86
    flat, for belay anchors, *85*
    natural anchors and slings using, *5*
    for quad belay anchor systems, *96*
    for sliding X belay anchors, *92, 95*
    toproping rigging with, *118*
    tying instructions, *62*
    See also BHKs (big honking knots)

P

parsimony, law of, 73
pear-shaped locking carabiners, *72, 80,*
    93, 99, 111
Petzl
    autoblocking devices, *103, 111*
    belay devices, *111, 112, 113*
    edge protectors, *128*
    hangers, *43*
    quick links, *135*
pockets, as natural anchors, *11, 12,*
    35, 40
pollution, visual, *49*
Powers Company
    contraction bolts, *44, 48, 138*
    expansion bolts, *43, 44, 49, 118*
    history, *43*
    for rappel anchors, *134, 138*
pre-distributed (equalized) anchor
    systems
    for belay anchors, 54, *55, 78,* 86,
        87, 105, 116
    cordelettes for, 76
    definition, 73
    for Joshua Tree System, *124*

for rappelling, *137*
primary placements, 42, 71, 73, 74, 75, 142
prusik knots, *67, 124*

Q

quad belay anchors
   composite anchors with, *104*
   rigging for, *97, 98, 99, 100, 101, 102, 103*
   tying instructions, *96*
quickdraws, 22, *26, 35*
quick links, *134, 135, 138*

R

rappel anchors
   equipment for, *134, 135*
   rigging examples, *134, 135, 136, 137, 138, 140*
   safety assessments, 133, *138, 139*
   safety tips, 133
rappelling, 133, *142*
rap rings, *135*
Rawl bolts, *43, 44, 47, 48*
redundancy
   as anchor system evaluation principle, 73
   basic facts of, 71
   natural anchor examples, *2*
   rappel anchor examples, *135, 136*
   toprope anchor examples, 117
ring bends (water knots), 6, *61, 139*
rock assessments
   for cam placements, 30, *36*
   detached blocks and, 7, *7, 8*
   flakes and, 7, *13, 30, 31, 42*, 117
   guidelines for, 7, *7, 9*
   for nut placement, 13, *26*
   for rappel anchors, *139*
   for toprope anchors, 117
rock failure, *16*
rock horns, *8, 9, 10, 11*

rope (edge) protectors, *124, 128*
rope(s)
   butterfly-looped, *107*
   coiling method for carrying, *89*
   directions of pull and lines of, *59, 60*
   favorite brands of, 121
   periodic inspections of, 42
   toproping and edge protection of, 117, *124, 128*
   toproping rigging, 121

S

safety assessments
   bolts, *44, 47, 48*, 50
   hangers, *46, 47, 49*, 50
   rappel anchors, fixed, 133, *138, 139*
   See also rock assessments
self-adjusting anchor systems, 73. *See also* sliding X
shock loading, 73
simplicity, as anchor system evaluation principle, 73
SLCDs (spring loaded camming devices), *19*, 42, *81*. *See also* cam placements
sliding X
   angles and, *90*
   basic information on, 90
   basics of, 98
   composite anchors with, *104*
   for Joshua Tree System rigging, *126*
   rigging, *90, 91*
   toproping anchors using, *120*
slings
   assessments of fixed, *139, 140, 141*
   for cam placement backup, *35*
   cam placements and basketed, *37*
   natural anchor examples, *4, 5, 11*
   natural anchors and threaded, *11*
   oppositional nut rigging and tensioning with, *21*
slipknots, *10*

SMC Company, *46, 49, 135*
solid, as anchor system evaluation
    principle, 73
SOS (nut placement acronym), 13
spinners, *48,* 50
SPORT (cam placement acronym), 30
spring loaded camming devices
    (SLCDs), *19,* 42, *81. See also* cam
    placements
stacked nut placements, *17*
stacked sliding X anchor systems, *93*
Sterling *Safety Pro* (rope), 121
stopper knots, 133
STRANDS Principle, 73–74, 108
submarine anchors, *98*
swing, 57

T
"tat," *141*
tensile strength, 6
threads, *11, 12, 139*
timely, as anchor system evaluation
    principle, 73
toproping anchors
  building guidelines, 117

rigging examples, *92, 97, 102, 103,*
    118, 119, 120
Totem Cams, *38, 39*
trees, as natural anchors, *2,* 3, *4, 5, 6*
triangle rigging, 79, *79,* 133, *136*
tricams, *27, 28*
triple fisherman's knots, *63*
tube devices, *103, 111*
tunnels, as natural anchors, *11, 12, 139*

U
upward oppositional belay anchors, 105,
    105, 106

V
V rigging, *78,* 79, *80, 136, 137*
V-slots, *23*

W
"walking" of cams, 29, 30
water knots (ring bend), 6, *61, 139*
webbing strength categories, 6
wedge bolts, *43, 44*
Wild Country Friend (cam), 29, *32*
Wild Country Rock (nut), *15, 18*